The Su

The Sun Will Shine Again

by

Cheryl Marie

The Sun Will Shine Again

Scripture quotations are taken from the New International Version (NIV) Copyright © 1973, 1978, 1984, 2011 by Biblica, Inc. All rights reserved worldwide.

What you are reading is based on the real life experiences of the author. The names of those involved have been changed to protect their actual identity.

Printed by KDP in the United States of America

Printing Edition 2019

Publisher KDP

ISBN paperback: 9781672400718

ISBN ebook: 9781670158260

Cover photos: Joelle Watt Photography

Cover design: Joelle Watt

Author photo: Joelle Watt Photography

Author Website: www.CherylMarie.net

Acknowledgements

To my devoted husband, Bill, who faithfully stood by me as I worked through the deep dark valleys of mental and physical pain. Your understanding, your care, your dedication, your willingness to draw closer to God and to me has transformed both of us and made our marriage stronger and our love deeper. You are the kind of man that I have wanted all my life. Your Godly attributes have truly blessed me and our home is a haven of peace and love. You are a wonderful husband and a precious gift from God. I love you with all my heart.

To all my beautiful and treasured children, who I love so much. I pray you will always know how important and special you are to me and to God. I am so sorry for the pain my decisions have caused you. I ask for and pray that you will grant me understanding and forgiveness. I also pray you will learn much from my mistakes and will always listen to and heed the voice of the Holy Spirit. Know your value in Christ and never allow anyone to treat you with any less respect than you deserve. Ask for divine wisdom before you make any decision and pay attention to and follow His leading. It will save you much heartache. In full and earnest pursuit, chase after God and your dreams. I believe in you, and nothing could ever change how much I deeply love you, my wonderful blessings from God.

To my mom, who is always there when I need her. In the last thirty years, I have learned what an amazing woman you are! I feel so much sorrow and compassion for you and for all the years you suffered in much the same ways as I did. Your strong will and relentless determination to rebuild your life and be independent has been such an example and an inspiration to me. Your support through all the struggles I have had has meant so much. Thank you for being a mother to my children when I was unable to care for them. Thank you for being my angel and staying by my side, nursing me back to health. You are such a blessing in my life and I thank God for you. Love you, Mom.

To my special friend, Jalynne Lewis, for the hours you spent going through my work in progress. Thank you for your guidance, your expertise, your honest critique, and your superb editing skills. I appreciate your encouragement and your beautiful heart as we cried together working on this book. God led me to you and because of His direction and your willingness to share your talents, I am your fellow author! I love you and thank God for you!

To my daughter, Jillian, for your willingness to climb down a rugged hillside to take the picture I had envisioned for the back cover of this book. You captured the sunlight in such a perfect way on top of the cliff for the front. Thank you for taking time from your busy photography business to snap my author picture. Most of all, thank you for the hours you spent, using your God-given talents, to create the perfect cover for my story. I love you and you are amazing!

To my daughter, Sheila, for the hours spent listening to and perfecting my story. Thank you for asking the hard questions and for helping me to express myself in a way that will touch hearts more effectively. I appreciate your willingness to help make this book the best it can be! I love you and you are brilliant!

To my sisters, Marsha, Dee, and Rose, who whole-heartedly supported my decision to expose our early years. We all lived in the same environment, but because of our age difference and our order of birth, we all have different perceptions. Your trust in me to tell the truth from my viewpoint as the oldest sibling has meant so much. I value my relationship with you and I thank God that we all are alive and well and serve Jesus. I love each of you so much.

To Sue, my God-sent, trustworthy, and supportive friend. Thank you for all the times that you reassured me to continue writing my story when I was struggling with doubts. Thank you for believing in me and listening to my frustrations. Thank you for knowing everything about me and accepting me just as I am. Your encouragement has made this book a reality. I love you and I am so grateful for your friendship.

To my Lord and Savior, Jesus Christ, my sure foundation and the rock on which I stand. In my testimony, I pray that I have lifted you high and have pointed to you as the answer to every problem in life. I pray I have presented you in such a way that others will desire a relationship with you and have effectively expressed that You are the reason I am alive today. Thank you for loving and protecting me through every trial and storm. Thank you for dying for me and forgiving me of all my failures. Continue to guide and direct my paths and I will follow you until the day when I join you in my heavenly home. All honor and glory is yours forevermore!

Dedication

To every person suffering with any type of pain. Do not be discouragd, but encouraged. Don't look at your overwhelming situation, but look to your awesome God who is bigger than any circumstance you may face. Know that the Lord is your healer and He answers prayer. Never give up on God for He is faithful and never fails!

Table of Contents

Foreword

Pain is a part of life and there is not a person alive that hasn't experienced some type of struggle either mentally, spiritually, emotionally, or physically.

About ten years ago, the Lord impressed on my heart to write a book about my experiences. Over the years, as I prayed and waited for the Lord's guidance, I had many questions. How could I do it? When should I write it? How much should I tell? Who would want to read it? What was the purpose?

I picked up my computer and began to type. The words began to flow as the Holy Spirit spoke to me. It was the same way every time I added to my work.

About one year ago, I knew that it was time to finish the book. I continued to write all that the Spirit gave me. The flow never stopped. This book is not my effort to share my pain, but a word picture of God's miraculous healing power.

My story is a story to all who are hurting. It doesn't matter what kind of situation in which you find yourself. It could be a separation, divorce, a damaged relationship with a friend or a family member, or even a disease or a sickness that has plagued you for many years. Possibly depression, oppression, a mental illness, or a disability. It could be rejection, loss, loneliness, or despair. It could be financial difficulties or social ostracism.

Life can be a real struggle. At times you have no hope. Frustrated, you feel like no one could possibly understand where you are or what you are going through. I want to tell you that I feel your pain, but more importantly, Jesus feels your pain. Only a prayer away, He is the answer for all your heartache.

I believe it is no accident that you are reading this book. God has allowed it to fall into your hands and I am honored to share my experience and my faith with you. My testimony is one of intense mental and physical pain, of utter despair and agony, of wrong choices and the resulting consequences, and at times, unbelievable hopelessness. More importantly, it is a story of Christ's constant care and His answers to the cries from deep within our being. I have included poetry that the Lord inspired me to write (some of which I have since made into songs) while in the deepest pit of my life. I pray that they will help you feel the depth of pain I experienced and understand more clearly the miracle that God has done for me.

"When you are happy, you enjoy the music. But when you are sad, you understand the lyrics." Unknown

My purpose in writing this book and my heart's desire is to take the lessons I've learned, the strength I've gained, and the testimonies I have experienced and impart hope to many who may be struggling with the cares of this life. If you carry your burdens alone, your way leads to a hopeless end. If you cast your burdens on Him, His way leads to an endless hope.

I cannot keep the goodness, mercy, and grace of my Lord to myself. I want to tell everyone I can about how Jesus Christ has not only been there for me, but has miraculously changed my life.

"I do not hide your righteousness in my heart; I speak of your faithfulness and saving help. I do not conceal your love and your faithfulness from the great assembly." Psalm 40:10 (NIV)

Beautiful pictures are developed from

negatives in a dark room.

So if you see darkness in your life,

be reassured that a beautiful picture

is being prepared.

Unknown

Chapter 1

The Dreaded Butcher Knife

I was a toddler in a dimly lit room. My dimpled hands gripped the bars of my crib, as I wailed at the top of my lungs. No comfort or consolation was offered from the person in the room. I do not recall what startled me so terribly, but I do re-member my heart racing and my heavy breathing as fear tight-ened every muscle in my body.

Fear was my constant companion. At a very young age, I experienced and learned fear while living in my home. There was no love, no peace, no happiness, no security; just turmoil and fear. I learned what I lived.

The colors and the arrangement of the furniture in the old, gray, wooden house we rented from the tailor in our neighbor-hood remain the same as the scene plays in my mind over and over again. The spotless kitchen included a red and white table with padded chairs trimmed with shiny chrome. A plastic covered red couch and chair, a green recliner, a blonde wood console black and white Zenith TV with rabbit ears, a blonde glass-topped coffee table and two matching end tables filled the small living room.

There are my parents…fighting again!

My father was scheduled to work at the local steel mill as a millwright from three to eleven that day. I felt relieved that for eight hours, there would be no screaming. But Dad had upset my mother again and she was seething with rage.

I was the oldest and both parents used me as a sounding board.

When he left the house for work, Mom's irritation and frustration were out of control. "I am going to stab him with this butcher knife when he gets home from work tonight," she screamed. Fear terrorized me and I began sobbing. "No! No! No!" I cried. "Please don't hurt Daddy!" I begged. "Please don't, Mommy, please, please, please!" I pleaded. My crying triggered something in her and before I knew it, she grabbed me and pushed me up against the wall. I felt the point of that dreaded butcher knife on the smooth and tender flesh of my little neck. "Shut up and stop crying or I will cut your dad in pieces tonight and use this on you, too!" she warned. I believed her. She finally released her grip on me and I ran to a corner and crouched for hours behind the big green recliner, shivering with fear. The rest of the day, I tried to think of a way to save my dad. If I failed, his death would be my fault.

That evening I went to bed with Marsha, my little sister. We could hear sounds throughout the house since there were no interior doors, except for the bathroom. We shared a double bed and the head was in view of the other bedroom where my parents slept. I said nothing to her about the dilemma. There was no need to scare or worry her. She was just a three-year old little baby. I was six and the oldest so I needed to handle this myself. It was my responsibility to keep peace in this family.

While Marsha slept, I stayed awake for hours, my little eyes burning like fire. I heard the squeak of the old wooden screen door and the turn of the lock on our interior door as my father entered our home. The thud of the closed door and the clack of the dead bolt assured me that he was in safely. The smell of his dinner and my nervous stomach made me nauseous. I heard the clink of the utensils as he ate his meal. In the background was the clear, monotone male voice of the announcer of the late-night news. I had no idea where my mother was or what she was doing. Time was crawling along, the possible last moments of my father's life. *I had to do something! What could I do?* My mind was racing.

I heard my dad go into the bathroom to get ready for bed. As I waited, my heart thumped so hard that I thought it would jump out of my chest. Finally, I heard the squeak of the bathroom door. He was ready for a good night's rest. As I saw my daddy walk past my bed, I knew I needed to warn him. I wanted to grab his arm and stop him from going into that room he shared with Mom, but I was frozen in fear. I was paralyzed. I couldn't speak.

As he crawled into bed, I turned to lie on my side so I could keep my sleepy stinging eyes glued on him. I could see the moonlight coming through the white blind on the top part of the open screened window by his bed. I became mesmerized as I lay watching and waiting.

As if out of nowhere, I saw my mother's silhouette in the moonlight. She raised the dreaded butcher knife over my father who was lying in bed. I screamed with all I had in me to arouse my dad. A struggle for that knife began. I continued to scream, hysterically, as they thrashed and wrestled for the control of the sharp knife. My dad was finally able to get it out of my mother's grip. She ran out of their bedroom, past me, swearing and threatening me for warning my father.

I was shaking and sobbing uncontrollably. My dad stayed in his bed and never said a word of consolation. I had no idea where my mother was. Marsha had slept through the whole ordeal. Now, I had to fear for my life all night long. *Would she come back and kill me?* No one was there to comfort me. No one was there to put their arms around me and make me feel safe. I was so frightened and confused. I thought all children were responsible for saving their daddy from a brutal stabbing. *What did I do wrong?*

I didn't sleep a wink that night. I couldn't move. The silence was haunting. *How could I handle the ongoing hatred my mother had for me because of my loyalty to my dad that night?* Even so, I wouldn't change what I had done.

MumMum

In spite of my terror-filled early years, my grandmother provided stability and love in my life. MumMum, who we visited a couple Sundays a month, was one of the few people that I really felt loved me and accepted me, in spite of the terrible child that I was. I was the worst; the most pitiful, the most despicable, the most undesirable offspring one could ever have produced. That was me and I knew it was true because my mother told me so. It had to be true because my dad would just toss me aside like a piece of trash when I did something that displeased him in some way. But my grandmother, oh she was a different story. I would run into her arms and she would embrace me and kiss me and tell me I was beautiful and what a good girl I was. Is it any wonder that I loved her so much and prayed every day that I might be able to live with her?

One of the days following the assault on my father, he had gone to work. I was busy playing house and mothering Marsha as my mom was talking on the phone with my MumMum. I overheard her calling me vulgar names and saying I was ugly, long-legged, and rotten. She told my grandmother how she wished I had never been born, that she hated my guts and she was going to kill me. I had heard these exact words all my life, but that day was the day my spirit was totally crushed because she was saying that to my grandmother, my hero. *How could she? My grandmother was the only person who loved me and now she was ruining it all! Now I have no one! And what did I do to deserve this?* I didn't understand! It hurt so bad! Even though I had never been willfully disobedient, I always ended up receiving the brunt of her wrath.

I worried so much about the next time I would see my MumMum. I felt ashamed, but I couldn't understand why. I wanted to die so I wouldn't have to bear the pain of rejection from the only person that cared about me. *No one in the whole world loves me now! I have no one!* My heart was broken!

When we visited MumMum on the following Sunday, I didn't run into her arms like I usually did. Slipping past her, I went into another room by myself. I couldn't face her. *How could my mother do this to me? How could she make my grandmother believe that I was so terrible? How could she ruin my life like this?* I was so sad and alone. What seemed like hours, but was only a few minutes, my MumMum came looking for me. Without a word, she embraced me in her arms and told me how much she loved me. I could do nothing but sob. No words were spoken about my mother's comments, but I knew she understood. *She still loved this horrible good-for-nothing child!*

I often wondered what it would have been like to just have one parent. We were celebrating my sixth birthday party at my grandmother's house. My mother dressed me in my favorite black and brown striped dress for my special day. I was sick with a high fever and an earache and napped on my grandmother's couch most of the day while the cousins were running about and playing in the same room. I was happy to be at my grandmother's house. Even though I was too ill to eat dinner, I couldn't wait to open my presents and eat some birthday cake and ice cream. My cousins sang "happy birthday." Then it came time to make a wish and blow out my six candles on my cake. My birthday request was not for a new bicycle, or the latest most popular toy, or a new baby doll to love and hug. As I pursed my lips and squished up my cheeks to squeeze my eyes closed tightly, I concentrated on my secret wish. *I wish that my parents would stop fighting. If that can't happen, I wish my daddy would leave and we could live alone with my mother or my mother would leave and we would stay with my daddy.* Then there would not be any more screaming and we would have peace in our house.

Since my mother's sister lived across the street with her seven children, my grandmother always had a lot of people at her house. I felt safer there than alone at home. I could escape from my living nightmare for a few short hours. I loved MumMum's large dresser with the long, heavy top drawer filled with trinkets and tiny toys and treasures. Each time I opened it, I would spend hours examining each one and arranging them in a neat orderly way just to come back a few weeks later and have to do it all over again. My many cousins discovered this dresser also and weren't as concerned with the neatness of this special drawer. But I had to make sure everything was in its place, just like at home. It was my responsibility to maintain order about everything I could. I had learned well.

Being the oldest of all the cousins, I would look for things I could do to help out, even at my grandmother's house. I loved to take care of my younger cousins all day. My Aunt Doris would marvel at my ability as a seven-year old and would give me a compliment by saying, "You take such good care of my babies, Cheryl. You are such a good little mother!" She would not even have to check on her children for hours as I would care for them, feed them, diaper them, and amuse them. It was my way of playing house and having a happy family and being a very kind and loving mother. In my imaginative play, I entered a pretend place where I could escape the pressure and dysfunction of my life. My make-believe "home and family" existed in a fantasy world where love flowed like a mountain stream refreshing all who would partake of its peace, where the sky was always blue, and the birds were always filling the air with beautiful melodies of tranquility. It was probably good therapy for me to have had this opportunity to share the love I had inside. I didn't ever have a chance to do that at home.

I made sure that I was available to help set the table for suppertime. We always had a crowd at MumMum's house. When times were hard for her, my mother would graciously bring all the food for this meal and everyone there would eat as much as they wanted. I loved being part of mealtime with a large family. I loved hearing conversation as everyone enjoyed the meal. It was so different than our meals at home where not a word was said and my father would sit with his back turned to my mother. Anything he needed, he asked me to ask her. I was so nervous that I couldn't eat and if I did, I would be sick at my stomach. I was very thin and anemic most of my childhood, but on Sundays at MumMum's, the food tasted good!

One of my favorite things to do was to read. I was a very smart child and would be able to read and comprehend books that were well beyond my grade level. As I got lost in the pages, I would find myself escaping from my reality. While I visited my grandmother's, I would sneak her big family Bible that she kept on the table in the "pink" room in her home. I would hide behind the big recliner in that room right on top of the old heat vent that periodically delivered blasts of warm air. As I read the thin delicate pages of her Bible, my mind and heart were like a sponge just soaking up all the beautiful promises in that precious book. I was especially stirred and encouraged to learn about the love that God, my Creator, had for me; so much that He sent His Son, Jesus to die in my place.

My grandmother and God loved me and I wanted to be as close to both of them as I could. I drew the conclusion that if she had God's book, she must be very special to Him.

Very rarely, I would get to stay over at my grand-mother's house and sleep in her big feather bed with her. What love I felt! How she adored me! I loved cuddling with her and feeling so safe. I loved her big smile and hugs when I came downstairs in the morning. Smells of warm toast and elderberry jelly still accompany my memories of her house. She was also known to all the neighborhood children as MumMum. They would come by to visit and knock on her rickety old wooden screen door and she would make room around her big table in her not so big kitchen. She would feed them with the little she had and would love on them. Sometimes I would feel a little jealous. She was my MumMum! I wanted her all to myself.

If I was really lucky, I would get to stay over on a Saturday night. I would even get to go to church with her on Sunday morning! Together in the front seat, we would ride the few blocks in her old turquoise car that she called "Gunga." What an interest I had in her church service. It was quite different than mine. They actually read from the Bible. I would just enjoy being with her and sitting next to her in God's presence.

Because of all the family members gathered together on Sundays, I did not feel so all alone. My stress during the visits to my grandmother's house was minimized, but not gone. My father watched my mother to make sure that she didn't even look the direction of any man that may be at the table. She was forbidden to even talk to her own brother-in-law and if he spoke to her, I would notice that she never looked at him when she answered. Even so, many trips home from MumMum's house would be terrible as the fighting and accusations engulfed the limited space in our small car. Terrorized, I asked God to protect us. We arrived home safely, only to endure all night fighting, screaming, and violence, and then silence; deadly silence. My mother would always be mean to us because of the tension created by the ridiculous demands of my father. I figured that out even at seven years old.

I loved visiting because Aunt Paula, my mom's step-sister, lived with my MumMum. She was just three years older than me. I idolized her and would hibernate for hours with her in her locked bedroom while my sisters and cousins pounded on her door, but were denied entrance. I felt so privileged to hang out with her and her friends. I admired all the Pirate banners hanging on her walls, her majorette outfits, and her batons. One time, Aunt Paula and several of her friends invited me to play with them.

We were in the dark damp basement of my grandmother's home. It was summer and we went there to escape the hot sun. The humungous coal furnace filled the back part of the cellar. The laundry tub and the old wringer washer were on the one side. MumMum had her large ecru colored lacey table cloth stretched on the wooden curtain/tablecloth stretcher on the other side. There was a limited area for play. Since I was the youngest and was quite small for my age, the older girls decided to have some fun. One of Aunt Paula's friends held my arms and the other friend held my feet. They swung me back and forth. Without warning, my arms slipped out of the grip of the young girl and my head crashed onto the cement floor. It hurt really bad, but my biggest fear was that I wouldn't be allowed to play with them anymore. I don't remember it as a bad memory, but as a fun time with my Aunt Paula. That gloomy basement also was used for our variety shows. We would hang sheets on the clothesline for our curtain. The parents would come and watch as we performed dances, songs, and marching routines. During the hot summer days, I spent time on MumMum's shaded front porch on her cushioned glider with my favorite aunt's friends. On occasion, I was privileged to be included with a coed group for a trip to the theater to see a movie. We had to walk across a bridge over the Monongahela River to the next borough. A couple of the guys picked me up and pretended to throw me into the river below. It scared me so bad that to this day, I have a terrible fear of bridges and water. The honor of spending time with my Aunt Paula far outweighs any memory of fright and pain. How I looked up to her, even though I was jealous because she got to live with my grandmother.

Mom was a giving person. She would always make sure Aunt Paula had what she needed whether it be money or clothes. My grandmother had been married twice. Her first husband, my mother's father, was an alcoholic and a very abusive man. I never knew him. Mom said he made life miserable for my grandmother and the three children they birthed. She divorced him after many years and married Bruce, who was Aunt Paula's father. I didn't know him well either. My grandmother took care of Bruce, who suffered with throat cancer. They lived on government surplus food because of the lack of income. Bruce passed when Aunt Paula was thirteen years old. MumMum had a hard life, but I admired her strength and optimism, her deter-mination, her laughter, and the love that flowed from her heart no matter what the circumstances. I can still hear her reply when someone asked how she was doing. "Fine and dandy," she would chirp. I always thought, *I want to grow up and have a positive attitude like that! I want to love like she loves and be kind and cheerful to everyone no matter what the situation. I want to be just like my MumMum.* Mom would bring food, and toilet paper, and provide the things that Aunt Paula needed as a young teenager. My father would fix anything that needed attention, whether it be appliances, the wooden porch, or the car.

Even though my life at home was chaotic, I now see that both my father and mother expressed their love by giving and doing things for others. That is the only way they knew how to show their feelings. They had giving hearts. They weren't bad people at all, just very dysfunctional in their relationship. They were toxic together.

Chapter 3

The Never-Ending Grip of Fear

"Do not be far from me, for trouble is near and there is no one to help." Psalm 22:11 (NIV)

Because mealtime in my home was so stressful, my appetite was ruined and my food was often left on my plate. I became anemic and had to get physical exams and blood tests regularly to check iron levels. Traumatized every time I visited the doctor, I screamed and cried and had to be held down by nurses. I would leave spitting mad at my parents, the staff, and the patients in the waiting room. Even the lollipop they gave me did nothing to change the way I felt about everyone in that whole office.

When I was eight years old, Dee was born. Soon after, our family moved to another house in the same neighborhood. It was a larger home, but still had only two bedrooms. Since I was the oldest,

I had my own twin bed while Marsha and Dee shared a double bed in the same room.

I trembled in my bed each night. Even though the covers engulfed me, I had no sense of security. From the top of my head to the tips of my tiny toes, my frail little body involuntarily convulsed. Sleep overtook me after endless hours of uncontrollable shaking. I was frightened by the sound of every settling crack in the old wooden house we called home. My nights were filled with terror as I anticipated the next violent fight between my parents. Apprehension and anxiety stole my peace as I slept. There was so much that could happen before the morning light shown through the windows. I stared at my little sisters sleeping peacefully in the big double bed across the room, aware that I had to be responsible for their safety.

In the warm weather, I felt the wind as it blew the plas-tic drapes through the open, screened window. My eyes were glued as the flames, shooting from the stacks of the steel mill in the valley below my house, cast large moving shadows on our bedroom wall, joining the dance with the drapes. I was paralyzed with panic, my imagination ran rampant, as I watched the flowing forms create giant hovering monsters that could swallow me up and take me away. I wondered if that journey would be better than staying at home. I didn't know which was worse, the shadows and sounds of the wind blowing in the summer or the black, threatening darkness and deathly silence in the winter when all the windows and drapes were closed. I drifted off to sleep, but I did not escape the reality of my life. It was hard to differentiate the nightmares at night from the real time events throughout the day.

The Desperate Prayer of a Frightened Child

Cheryl Marie

Little heart, trembling in fear;
Little face, covered in tears,
Little hands, folded in prayer-
Dear Jesus, are you there?

Send your angels to guard me tonight
And keep me safe till the morning light.
Tomorrow is another day-
I live each one in the same old way

I'm so scared for my mom and dad.
The fights they have-they get so bad!
I'm so small; what am I to do?
That's why, Jesus, I call on you.

Will I wake at the break of day?
Will I die? That's what I pray.
I live my life with this awful fear;
Please, oh, Jesus, stay very near

Fear encompassed all areas of my being for my whole life. I had a fear of people, especially those who should have been the closest to me. I feared the wrath I received when I failed to be the perfect child. I feared the rejection and silence I received from my father when I didn't do or say what he wanted. The silent tantrums would last for days or even weeks until I repeatedly begged for forgiveness for my unknown and significant failure. I feared my mother and the beatings, the screaming, the ugly, degrading name-calling, and all the other assaults on my developing self-esteem. I feared the threats of death if I didn't straighten up and be what I should be, whatever that was. I feared the criticism when I didn't get straight A's on my report cards. After all, my achievements would reflect on their success as parents! An added fear was my mother's threat of a man who watched me through the window. She told me and had me believing that he would whisk me away when I failed to please her in any way. The truth is that I could have never met the expectations of either of my parents because they were far above my age and maturity. Most of their demands were not even in the normal realm of a young girl's life. I feared the assignments of taking thousands of messages back and forth between my parents. The only communication between them for the twenty years that I lived at home was done by me running back and forth with their disrespectful comments to each other. It was me who had to decipher the messages to make them easier to be received, leaving out choice words that I wouldn't repeat. It was me who heard the malicious anger, the unhidden disapproval, the bitter sarcasm, the intense hate, and the deadly threats as a response to the message I delivered. In turn, when I took one back, I heard the negativity all over again. I was expected to be the communicator, the peacemaker, and the problem solver of their dysfunctional marriage. I felt ignored and invisible until I was needed to deliver some derogatory communication.

I feared the bone-chilling silence that filled my days as my parents spoke to each other only a few times in my whole life. Their silence created a major roar in my home. The atmosphere was uneasy, thick with seething hatred and anger, filled with intense and undeniable tension. Even as a young child, I had to be prepared and on guard, never knowing at what moment of the day or night that the next battle would start. *What would happen? How would it end?*

I feared the nights of terror with the crying, the screaming, the filthy demeaning name-calling, the mortifying accusations, the sounds of metal against metal as the butcher knives were shuffled to find the biggest and the sharpest, the thrashing physical struggles, the slamming doors, and then, again, the silence. All this happening as my little sisters and I trembled in our beds, not knowing whether we would be orphans or even alive at daybreak.

I feared for my life and the lives of my sisters. *What would I do if they were physically injured? What could I do to save them if we were all in danger?* I feared that I would miserably fail them; then I would carry around the guilt my whole life. Instead of being a carefree child and playing with my toys and friends, my brain would be analyzing our life situation and figuring out a plan to escape just as one would do in case of a fire. I would be the one responsible for getting my sisters and me safely out of the house when the situation would arise. *But how would I do it? Where would I go? Who would I call? What would happen to us?*

I had a haunting fear of dying. Being the despicable child that I was told I was, I had a fear of going to hell to live with the devil. I was told in the church across the street that I attended that Satan and Jesus were always giving me a choice of right and wrong, almost as if each had their place on one of my shoulders. I had a choice to whom I would listen. This impacted me and I began to envision this scenario. I tried to do everything right, but it was drilled into my head that I did nothing right. I believed it. I imagined I saw him in the mirror-the devil, sitting on my shoulder, in all his red attire with his mean eyes and his protruding horns. I tried to avoid any mirrors in the house unless someone was close by. This developed an intense fear of doing anything wrong. I was programmed to think about every move I made and every word I said. I would pray for God to help me because I was told that I was no good, all bad, and would never grow up to be anybody worth anything. I assumed that I was the devil's child. A never-ending spiritual battle was being fought in my heart. I felt it all the time. I lived in hell itself. I fought as hard as I could to be close to God. He was the only hope I had. There was no way out except by a miracle or by death. I was just a little innocent child and was too young to run away. Besides, I couldn't leave my younger sisters behind. As the oldest, the decision had to be made. I would stay to protect them; I would ask God to protect us all.

Living was my greatest fear. Every hour of every day was overwhelming. After rising every morning, the day pro-ceeded downhill from then. I was either ignored or verbally attacked. I am not sure which was worse. Even though I spent my day avoiding any conflict, my stomach twisted with pain and my hands sweated and shook as I was forced to engage in my parent's "communication" games. I didn't understand the re-sponsibility I was carrying. *Why were they doing this to me? Why was life so hard? Why couldn't I just be a kid?* So many issues I worried about and my age hadn't even reached double digits!

What would my parents do to me if I let "the cat out of the bag" and finally told someone what life was really like between the walls where we lived? My little mind was boggled with questions such as these instead of what game should I play or what friend can I invite to my house.

In keeping up this charade of a happy normal family, I thought about the validity of my own feelings and perceptions. I had to live a lie about what I was thinking and feeling. I dare not give an opinion on anything for fear of taking sides and contributing to the fighting. Trying to play their games and staying on guard drained me of energy. Nobody could help me, even if they did believe what was going on in my life. Guilt overwhelmed me because I couldn't fix my parent's marriage.

I was expected to exist in pure hell in my home, keep it all a secret, and pretend that we were a normal happy family. I had the underlying fear that I would betray my parents if I told the truth. What would be the consequence? *Would they kill me? Would they send me away somewhere like my mother had always threatened me? Then who would watch over my sisters?* I had to continue to be silent and live the façade.

What a distorted sense of loyalty! A kid should never have to carry the responsibility that was laid on my shoulders.

Who was I? How could a mere child be forced into adult roles and responsibilities? Why was this all happening to me? It didn't feel right! It wasn't fair! It didn't feel good to have no time that I could be a normal kid!

A Picture of Perfection

Perfection-perfect marriage, perfect children, perfect home. That's what everyone thought as our family walked through town on Saturday afternoons in the fifties and sixties. That was the only day we left our meticulously clean and organized house, except for my father who worked a fulltime job at the local steel mill. On Saturdays, town was crowded and Marsha, Dee, and I would be paraded down the streets of town to do weekly shopping. Party dresses, curls bouncing around the matching ribbons in our hair, ruffled little socks, and shiny white leather shoes caused heads to turn in admiration. Not only did we look like we were entering a pageant, but our behavior was extraordinary. I heard the ooh's and ahh's and saw the stares from strangers along the streets and in the stores. My mother would shyly accept all the compliments for being an outstanding mother and my dad's shirt buttons nearly popped with pride. "What a perfect little family," everyone would say. "God has surely blessed you."

I sensed that something was very wrong with this picture. I wondered why they said that because the only mention of God in our house was when my parents would put the name of God or Jesus with other words that I wasn't allowed to say.

I continued to visit a small Catholic church near my home. I went every Sunday morning alone. I was drawn to the atmosphere of that little church and was awed by the reverence He was given. I lived a life of fear and uncertainty and that church was a place that gave me feelings of love, peace, and safety. I had not forgotten the beautiful promises in my grandmother's Bible that had deeply impressed my heart. Curious, I wanted to hear and learn everything I could about God. I needed Him and through childlike faith, I desperately reached out and clung to His love in the only way I knew how.

I didn't feel loved at home. I didn't feel peace, safety, security, acceptance, or happiness. Hatred, anger, fear, rejection, tension, unrest, insecurity, and an enormous amount of hopelessness was what I felt. I realize all these things now, but back then, I didn't really know what was normal. I was a little child with more responsibilities than most adults would ever have. I was in charge of all the communication in my parent's marriage, for all the decisions made in my home, and for the safety of my sisters and myself. I thought all parents acted like mine. I thought all moms and dads hated each other. I thought all parents didn't talk to each other. I thought all parents had violent fights all night. I thought all children were pounded, beaten, and slapped around for minor mistakes or even in anger and frustration that had nothing to do with them at all. I thought all children cried themselves to sleep each night. I thought all children had their spirits crushed and endured the pain of being called unspeakable, foul and filthy names. I thought all children were demeaned by derogatory remarks and hearing they were ugly and hated and were going to be given away. I thought all children had to fulfill parental obligations to their siblings. I thought all children miserably failed to do the right thing all the time. I thought all children were starved for affection and felt a big hole in their heart that ached for acceptance. I thought all fathers told their children that someday they would not come home from work and they may never see them again. I thought all fathers would go for months shunning their little children and not even tell them what they did wrong. I thought all parents didn't speak to each other for several decades. I thought the oldest child in all families was the appointed messenger between the mother and father. I thought all children woke trembling from head to toe in the middle of the night as they heard cursing, slamming, screaming, wailing, thrashing, name-calling, and death threats. I thought all children were constantly put in a position of judge and jury to decide the guilt of one or both parents. I thought all children shook in fear and gasped for breath all night wondering that if this time their mother would actually carry out the threat of suicide with the large sharp butcher knife that she routinely removed from the kitchen drawer. I thought everybody lived a farce and life was nothing like it really was behind closed doors.

The Door

Cheryl Marie

Behind the door, love turns to hate.
Behind the door, perfection turns to hell.

Behind the door, the picture glass is shattered
Nothing or nobody matters, behind the door.

I wonder what it's like beyond the door?
Is there a different world on the other side?
Do people talk, do people laugh, do people love?

I'll never know
For it's a place I cannot go
Beyond the door.

We were a perfect little family? Is that what we really were?
How could that be? There was something disturbing in my immature little mind. Something was just not right, but I was too young to know any better or to find the answers I needed. *How could we look like a picture of perfection and be this unhappy?* I resolved to think that all families were like mine.

Chapter 5

How I Hated Saturdays

I remember Saturdays. Even though I looked forward to them, I dreaded them. Saturday was the day when our family would do our weekly shopping and we had some sem-blance of "family time." But Saturday was also the day of the most violent feuding and fighting that I recall.

My father was of the Italian heritage and he had deeply imbedded and very distorted beliefs that impacted our family. My mother was forbidden to leave the house for any reason without him. She wouldn't dare step over the threshold of the doorway for fear of getting on the bad side of him. Any shopping during the week was my responsibility. I walked with my little note to the nearest store, which seemed like miles at my young age. I trudged up the long hill in the intense heat of summer, my arms overflowing with the necessities for the day. My mother was only permitted outside the door of our home for any relief from the tasks of homemaking on Saturdays.

Saturday was a day of turmoil because we all had to wait and see if my father was willing to take us out. He would spitefully sleep in late and take his time doing things around the house while we waited to see if we should get ready to go. I was forbidden to play outside with my friends until we knew what we were doing that day. Sometimes my playmates came and sat on our porch and talked to me for a while through the wooden screen door. Even though this helped to pass the time, I felt even more angry about the whole situation. I got up early and waited for what seemed like an eternity until, sometime late in the afternoon, it was decided we were or were not going. I wasted half my life waiting, my little stomach seeping acid from the stress of the long-awaited decision.

It was all a game between the adults in the family, but the anticipated waiting took its toll on my physical being. Many Saturdays were days of crying, screaming, accusations, violence and in the end my dad would finally decide. It was me who had to go and ask Dad if he was taking us and report back to my mother. It was me who had to deliver the negative answer. As a result, I stood and was screamed at with obscenities and bone-chilling threats of what was going to happen to him, my sisters and I because of his refusal to go. It was me who had to go and deliver these remarks to my father and back and forth I would go, shaking and crying with fear. Sometimes he refused to go and that meant endless hours of violent fighting through the night and days ahead. It was all my fault too because he told me no and I couldn't change his mind; no one could. But, if and when he said he would go, we would all proceed to get ready, only to wait endlessly for my dad.

Sometimes it took hours waiting in our Sunday best even though it was Saturday. We wouldn't dare move because we may mess our hair or dirty our shoes. We weren't allowed to eat or drink because we may spill something on us. My sisters and I sat, waiting, until finally dad emerged from the bedroom. It was time to leave. We appeared as a happy little family, all dressed to perfection going out to enjoy our Saturday shopping spree.

Into the car we would all go and I waited for my dad to question me where to drive. I asked my mom and she told me. I relayed the answer to my father. Back and forth. Back and forth, all day long.

So confusing for a small child.

Chapter 6

Great-Grandmother, Mom

On occasion, my family would visit my maternal great-grandmother on Saturdays when we were out walking on our facade through the streets of town. She had an apartment on the third floor, above a Chinese restaurant. As I walked up the steep steps, the Chinese men and women would look out and wave to us and comment to my mom and dad how beautiful their children were and what a nice family we had. These were the usual comments and I got so accustomed to hearing them, they did nothing for my self-esteem. The words seemed to go in one ear and out the other. I watched as my mother smiled and my dad proudly said "thank you." My parents thrived on these compliments.

The Chinese were very nice and I tried to get a peek into the restaurant each time we were there. I had never eaten Chinese food and the aroma of all the different kinds of food filled the stairway and made my mouth water. I thought the best part about visiting my great-grandmother was smelling the food when we opened the door and walked up the stairs to her apartment!

The next best part was looking out her huge windows at all the people walking the streets of town. There were big wide window seats with plump red velvet cushions and we girls sat there quietly looking at the sights. It seemed as though we were looking from an airplane even though we were only three stories high.

My great-uncle lived with my great-grandmother. He was a short, thin, undernourished, unshaved, hunch-backed man with wide baggy-legged pants pulled tight at his skinny waist with a wide and worn leather belt. His soiled white muscle shirt hung on his sunken chest and rounded shoulders. I recall the intense smell of body odor mixed with alcohol, his beady eyes, and his oversized Adam's apple that slid down his neck when he swallowed. Even though I never heard him speak a word, he scared me almost as much as my great-grandmother did.

I didn't care for my great-grandmother and I sensed that she didn't care for me or any of my sisters or cousins. Her large frame, was always seated in a large wicker rocking chair. Pure white, medium length, frizzy hair surrounded her face like she had stuck her finger in an electric socket. Piercing eyes and thin lips that never smiled told me to keep my distance. Her apartment was as eccentric as she was. Thick red velvet draperies that hung between the doorways of her large rooms were pulled shut to enclose a chamber of mystery. I still can hear the whispering, murmurings, and sobbing coming from that area. The mysterious, solemn, and eerie atmosphere used to send cold shivers up my spine. I shied away from any contact with Mom, which is what everyone called her. Mom gave me the creeps and my MumMum pulled me aside and encouraged me not to be afraid of Mom. She said my great-grandmother was very special to God and God told her things that He told no one else and she was His messenger to people on earth. I was puzzled. *If she was God's messenger, then why was she so unloving? And if she was my sweet MumMum's mother, how could she be so cold and stern?* I just wanted to get the visit over with as quickly as possible.

I grew to understand that Mom was a spiritualist, a mediator, one who contacts the dead and brings back messages to the living, one who predicts the future. My great-grandmother was involved in the Satanic world. It amazes me that I felt this discernment even as young as I was. I see now that God had His hand on my life and has protected me and claimed me as His child from the very beginning.

Childhood Memories

Freedom from responsibility, fun in the sun, sports, friend's birthday parties, sleepovers, playing in the dirt, family vacations, laughter, hugs, kisses, unconditional love, picnics, board games, family fun nights-oh, the greatness of being a kid! I can't identify! How could I identify! I felt like I was in a prison, not allowed to go outside and enjoy the day until noon or later and had to be in the house before dusk every day. This time was not all mine because I was called in every hour or so to report what I was doing and who I was with. Sometimes I had to mediate a "conversation" or relay information between my parents. I had to set the table for meals and do the clean up every day. It felt overwhelming. Because I had to help clean the house, I had very little time to play. How I longed to stay out to play kick the stick with all the kids on the block. They would gather together at the intersection of the neighborhood street about seven each evening and play. There was no traffic at that time. Everyone was home from work and the moms stood around watched the game and talked. My father made it clear that my mother was not allowed out of the house and was not permitted to have friends.

Even though the intersection was in sight of our house, my sisters and I had to go home. How I hated it! As I watched from the front porch, I felt like I was deprived of having any fun in my life. I was angry and embarrassed and had no way to express it. There was enough going on at my house and I dare not start any conversations about my needs. I had tried that with Mom and Dad and was reprimanded and told to do as they say! It was about their needs! It was all about their needs!

We never took a vacation. Occasionally, Dad told me to inform my mother that we were taking a day trip to a lake three and one-half hours away. We traveled in our blue Ford Falcon with no air conditioning, sitting on plastic see-through seat covers. It was so hot and the warm air blowing through the car windows did not cool us. Mom would pack sandwiches, cookies, fruit, and cold drinks and we would stop to eat at a road-side picnic area. The meal was as nerve-racking as it was at home. We arrived at the lake and my dad would go in the water with us while Mom sat in the sand nearby. We stayed a few hours and would endure the trip home. I hated those trips. I hated the unsettling silence in the car for such a long time. I have no good memories of family time on those dreaded outings!

In my early childhood, playing house with my treasured collection of baby dolls was one of my favorite pastimes. Each held a special place in my heart and I gave them each a name. I would dress them up in the variety of clothes that I accumulated for them and I combed their tangled matted hair the best I could. I loved to cuddle them and tell them how much I loved them. In our childhood make believe time, it was fine with me if one of my friends wanted to be the daddy, but I wanted to be the mommy. My dolls became a very important "family" to me.

While at play, I constantly worried about the safety of Marsha and Dee at home. I remember hopscotch, riding my bike, and skating. But I could never enjoy anything for long. What if a violent fight broke out and I wasn't there to protect my sisters! I had to stay close to the house.

I continued to attend that little Catholic church and be-came involved in the lessons offered for children my age. Church was very important to me and I took it seriously. I prayed the prayers I was taught continuously, almost desperately at times. I tried to reach God in the only way I knew. I figured out somewhere along the way that I could just talk to him instead of repeating those prayers that didn't make much sense to me. I wanted God to hear my heart. I wanted Him to know the pain I was experiencing, how scared I was to sleep, to live, to die. At times I felt peace when I prayed; At times I felt empty. I didn't know where to go, who to trust, what to believe, how to continue on. I felt so much confusion and fear and pain and I didn't know what to do with it all.

Children were seen and not heard in our house, especially when we were with other people besides our immediate family. I was never allowed to be in the presence of my grandmother, aunts, or uncles when they were talking about anything. I was never included and was ordered to "go play" whenever any conversation started. If I didn't scoot out of there as fast as I could, I would be embarrassed by being threatened and called a derogatory name. If my aunts and uncles visited our house, it was always late on Saturday evening after our day out. The visit would last until at least midnight, sometimes beyond. My mother was a very hos-pitable person and would put out a spread for our visitors. If cousins would come, we would all fall asleep on the floor and when the "party" was over and everyone would leave, I would be awakened abruptly out of a deep sleep and ordered to clean up the mess in the kitchen. *I was just a little child! How cruel can you be?*

We would stop in at my father's parents sometimes after our Saturday shopping spree. On occasions, my uncles would be there with their families and I would get to see my cousins. I hardly knew them because my father kept us away from all family functions because of his tight reins on my mother and her contact with other males. It didn't matter who they were. I always felt left out and like an outcast in everyone's presence. My Uncle Rudy was my dad's youngest brother and was a talented singer/musician. He was ten years older than me. I loved when he was home and was practicing his music. I would be mesmerized listening to him sing and play his guitar. I wanted to play the guitar, too. I wanted to sing, too. I was a natural at harmony. Most of my father's Italian family members were great singers. Some nights, everyone sat around and sang beautiful songs with harmonies. I was happy to be included. These were the occasions that I treasure, but they were few and far between.

Throughout our childhood, Marsha and I would sing to pass the time. I would learn every song from my music class at school and teach them to Marsha. After she would learn the melody, I would add harmony. I would then sing melody and Marsha would do harmony. We would sing in the car on our Saturday escapades. Our voices would break the uncomfortable silence in our vehicle. Music became a big part of our lives.

There was a single mother with two young daughters who lived two doors up the street from our house. She was pretty and dressed attractively just to sit on her porch. Dad liked her. It was apparent. Although my mother was not allowed out of the house, my dad had free reign to do as he pleased. He often worked on our car or a neighbor's car in the parking places in front of our house. He walked the neighborhood for exercise. He owned a small motorcycle that he enjoyed riding and taught me to ride also. He frequently chatted with this single mother. It made me uncomfortable to see Dad laughing and obviously enjoying a conversation with another female. He never talked to my mother. *Why was he so nice to her and fought with Mom?* The frequent fights about this woman were horrid, but Dad continued to spend time with her every chance he had.

Dickie was a seventeen-year-old boy in the neighborhood who was a hot shot and a show-off. He drove too fast and his muffler was too loud as he raced through the neigh-borhood streets. Concerned for their children's safety, many of the parents had reprimanded this boy about his reckless driving habits. It was July eighth and I was thirteen years old. I had been at my friend's house a block away from where I lived. I was walking home and I heard the loud squealing of tires and then a thump. As I looked up, I saw the rear end of Dickie's car high in the air as he slammed on his brakes. Underneath, lying in full view on the cement road right in front of our house, was my four-year old little sister, Dee. I was stunned, and then ran home screaming for my parents. My mom ran out to her and was hysterical beyond words. My dad, who was sleeping because he had to go to work that evening, stood dumbfounded on the front porch. I think he was dazed. Dee was lying in a pool of blood that came from the large deep gash on her head. The desperate cries of my mother, the blood, the exposed bone protruding from the gash and the stillness of Dee's tiny body caused my stomach to be sick and my knees to be weak. The blaring sirens of the ambulance completed the horrific scene. She was critically injured, her skull smashed and soft like a bowl of gelatin. The doctors didn't give her much hope and if she did survive, she would likely have brain damage. Miraculously, she did live. After coming home from the hospital, she had to lie flat on her back for months. I stayed by her side every day, all day, until she was well. I had to make sure she was safe. I believed it was all my fault because I wasn't watching out for her. I can still see that scene in my mind as if it happened yesterday.

Chapter 8

Teen Years-the Best Years of Your Life?

I noticed in Junior High School that I was different. I didn't fit in anywhere with anyone. I wasn't permitted to do the kinds of things that most kids do at that age. School dances were out of the question! No PJ parties, no hanging out at friend's houses, no football games. *For Pete's sake! They were on Saturday afternoons in the broad daylight!* This is when I started to feel the tinge of deep-rooted anger down inside of me. How I longed to fit in and just go to a football game! But it was Saturday and that was the day I had to be head communicator for our weekly downtown walk!

I made good grades in school, but I was lonely and needed acceptance like kids do at that age and I found none. Several teachers would take the time to talk to me and to compliment me. Desperate for their kindness, I instantly became very attached to them and looked forward to seeing their smiles, to catch a wink, or to have an arm around my shoulder. God knew what I needed in my life and He was so faithful and used other people to minister to me.

A small group of friends who sat together at lunch hung out at each other's houses on Friday evenings. I wasn't allowed to take part, even for a few hours, because that group included boys and my father did not allow boys in my life. He would put the male sex down and say they were all no good. All boys had dirty minds and were after one thing. He was glad he didn't have sons; he never wanted a son. Over his dead body would I date anyone as long as I was in his house.

Randy was a clean-cut young man who was soft spoken and respectful. Randy was kind to me and ate lunch next to me. How I looked forward to lunch every day. Randy wrote me notes and slipped them to me as we passed in the halls between classes. My first love! So special; so exciting! How wonderful it would have been to be able to talk about Randy at home and have him come over and spend time at my house. How I wanted to go to the football game with him! There wasn't a Friday that Randy didn't ask me to do something with him. I always had to say no. How my heart hurt; I thought I would die! Randy called me every night on the telephone and my parents would not leave the room and told me to get off the phone every few seconds. I hated them for that. Randy became frustrated. He started to come by my house with a couple of friends on Friday evenings. His goal was to meet my parents. He hoped they would see that he was a decent kid. When he knocked on the door, Dad or Mom told him sternly that I couldn't come to the entry or talk to him. How embarrassed I was! I eventually lost my first love because of my parents. That was the pattern for all my relationships until I graduated high school. Bitterness and anger filled my heart.

I planned to run away. Anything would be better than to live like I had to live. I planned what I would do and where I would go. I went over my plan with determination, but I knew I could not leave my sisters in that horrible atmosphere. I had to endure and protect them. Eventually, I just gave up on friends. I gave up on boyfriends. I gave up on dances and parties and football games. I accepted my situation in my personal prison just to keep peace.

Things were really bad at home. Getting older, I began to realize the severity of the situation and what could really happen during my parent's fights. As I laid in my bed at night and waited for the argument to escalate to violence, my heart pounded and my body sweated profusely as I shivered uncontrollably. My stomach churned and my mouth became dry as I breathed in short shallow breaths so I could concentrate on every sound that came from the downstairs. I had to be ready to guard my sisters and myself! *What would I do? How could I keep us safe?* There were times when I somehow got pulled into the battle and had to protect myself physically and verbally. I had a roof over my head, food in my stomach and clothes on my back. For these things I was thankful, but I would have given them up for just a real home, some love in my life, a place where I could feel safe, protected, accepted, and respected. I had none of that. I was so sad and had a constant gnawing ache in my heart.

My mother birthed my youngest sister when I was sixteen. I named her Rose. Gossip spread that she was my illegitimate child. That didn't bother me in the slightest. She couldn't have been mine because I wasn't allowed to date or even mention the opposite sex in my home. I was denied a normal life. After Rose was born, my days revolved around her needs. I was thrilled to have someone else to lavish with love. I bathed, fed, and nurtured her, I played with her and took her for walks. I protected her. I raised her. I lived for her. I would die for her. My heart yearned for children of my own and I loved Rose as much as I could ever love my own child.

January eighth will be forever etched in my mind. It was seven at night and I was upstairs in our two-bedroom home working on my homework. Marsha and Dee were downstairs taking the lights and ornaments off the Christmas tree. Rose was sleeping on the couch in the living room located in the front of the house. I was dressed in cut off short green jeans and a white shirt, no socks or shoes. I heard screams and a strange roaring sound. As I jumped from the bed and opened the bedroom door, flames were licking the walls of the steps. Without a second thought, I raced down the burning staircase and found the dining room, where the tree was located, engulfed in a raging fire. My mother was outside with Marsha and Dee, yelling to me that Rose was still inside. My dad overheard my mother and he dashed up the now blazing stairway to rescue her. Without thinking, I ran back inside the side door, past the stairway and went to the living room and found Rose, my heart and soul, sleeping on the couch. I took her outside, unharmed, through the front door of the house. My father was still inside and the firemen couldn't go back in through the door. As they were getting a ladder to get to the upstairs of the home, my dad broke through the glass of the bedroom window and fell out onto the roof, barely conscious. I yelled to him that Rose was safe. All his facial hair was singed, his skin had minor burns, and he inhaled a lot of smoke, but would be fine. I learned something that day; even though Dad contributed to our home being a living hell, he loved us!

After the fire at our house, we had to move in with my beloved MumMum and her new husband, who became our grandfather. I went to get my driver's license because now I had a new responsibility. I was needed to taxi my sisters and myself to and from school and my father to and from work. My mother stayed all day with my grandparents at their home. Soon enough, my father alleged that my mother and grandfather were "up to no good." There was a tremendous fight and we packed up and left. This was an absolutely ridiculous accusation and was one of the worst days of my life. I will never forget the pained expression on my grandmother's face as her sad eyes welled up with tears and the helplessness she must have felt as we were pulled away from her. *How could my dad accuse my mother of such a thing? How could he hurt my MumMum like that? Wasn't losing our home and all our belongings enough? MumMum was the only security we had left!* That was the last day that my father ever spoke to her or my grandfather.

We moved into an old, bug-infested apartment building-very little clothing, very little food, and no furniture. My parents somehow obtained some used pieces-beds, kitchen table and chairs pots and pans, dishes, and bureaus. It was a terrible time, day in and day out with no escape.

I was very attracted to CJ, a young man I met on the bus that I rode to school. As I boarded, he would be sitting two rows back on the right side. Although we had never met, he greeted me very day with a sheepish smile and a wink. I learned that he was a year ahead of me in school and a foster child. It didn't matter. I was attracted to him. I wanted to date him, but I knew my father would not hear of it!

CJ and I talked every day on the bus to and from school. I learned about his life before and after his foster experience. He was the oldest of two children. The death of his sickly mother when he was fifteen marked the end of his family as he knew it. His sister was six and he had been her responsible caretaker. His absent father was an alcoholic. Because none of the family volunteered to raise them, CJ and his sister were separated and placed in institutions. He told me about the painful day that happened, his little sister screaming and clawing his arms as she was dragged away. They were taken to different cities and had no contact except an occasional phone call.

The home for boys, where CJ was placed, was in my town. Al, a maintenance man at the home, befriended CJ. After getting to know him better, he invited CJ to his home for dinner and to meet his wife, Goldie. The couple bought CJ things he needed and liked. They invited him to their home on weekends. When CJ was seventeen, Al and Goldie became his foster parents.

CJ was excited and ready for the adjustment to a real home and family. He quickly sensed that Goldie ruled the house and Al, a very laid back and quiet man, would go along with anything she said just to keep peace.

Things went well for several months, even though CJ felt smothered. Because she had never had any children, she treated CJ like a little child. She would make him uncom-fortable with inappropriate affection, she tucked him in bed every night at his appointed bedtime, made him follow childish rules, picked out his clothes, and demanded he spend all his free time with her.

The day came when CJ told her about me. She didn't take it well. She limited his phone calls. She listened to his conversations. When she realized he was serious about me, she became jealous. She demanded he break off our relationship.

CJ turned eighteen. Goldie bought a car for his birth-day, but it was not his car. It was hers. They had never owned a vehicle and neither knew how to drive. The car was a tool to manipulate CJ to do anything she wanted. The tension grew as CJ began to resist her micro-mothering.

My family was still living in that horrible, depressing apartment. Life was hard. I was sneaking out to see CJ anytime I could muster up some lie about where I was going. I felt so guilty, but I had no other choice.

CJ's senior prom and graduation was fast approaching. He had asked me to his prom months before. I knew I wouldn't be allowed to go. I wanted to go more than anything. I was desperate. Aunt Paula was now married with a child and she and I were still close buddies. I talked to her about the prom and she said she would help me convince my parents to give me permission to go. I don't know what she said, but my dad reluctantly said I could go. Prom night was their introduction to the guy to whom I had been secretly talking and seeing. I was stressed anticipating CJ's arrival. Aunt Paula answered the knock on the door. CJ greeted my mother and under the watchful eye of my dad, she didn't look at him or respond. He reached out his hand to shake my father's. Dad stood with his arms crossed on his chest and looked right past him. Aunt Paula stepped forward and greeted CJ warmly. I felt physically ill and needed fresh air. Aunt Paula snapped a few pictures and we left. We tried to enjoy the short prom date in spite of the damper put on the evening. We had a picture taken, danced a few slow dances, and talked with friends. I was instructed to return straight home promptly and was not permitted to go to the after-prom picnic held the next day.

That summer, CJ started working a seven to four job in a sign shop. Most nights I talked to him on the phone, even though it was a short conversation with no privacy from either family. CJ tried to jump through all the hoops his foster mother created so that he could earn a few hours of use of the car. I then had to generate a believable plan to see him without the knowledge of my parents. The stress made us wonder if it would be easier to just forget we ever met.

Realizing our dilemma with our parents would not change no matter who we dated, we decided to continue our relationship. I was busy with school and caring for Rose and CJ worked every day. We talked often and arranged secret meetings when we could.

My parents were looking for a home for us. We all hated that wretched apartment. Since there was no communication between them, it was me who had to make this happen. Each day when the newspaper arrived, I would see each of them looking through the real estate ads and each would circle their picks. My job would be to go back and forth between them deciding which houses we would view. I would then call and arrange the appointments. After we looked, it was my job to get the feedback from both parents and relay to each of them what the other thought. Thank the Lord, we only looked at a few! My mother fell in love with a brick two-story with a large front porch facing a busy street. We would have neighbors and would be close to the schools we attended. My dad preferred a cape cod situated on a large plot of land. It was the only house on that side of the road. There was a steep hillside of trees that extended the whole side of the street behind the house and all the property. At least half the front had a hillside, covered with bushes and vegetation, that steeply sloped to the red brick street. There were no children in the neighborhood for my sisters to befriend. Again, we were separated from people in general. Dad, who liked his privacy, told me this house was where we would be moving. Mom had no say.

My senior year was spent conveying thousands of messages back and forth about that house. Many decisions had to be made as Dad beautified it. Coved ceilings were added to the plastered walls. The already shiny woodwork and doors contributed to the charm. A brown, orange, and tan velvet couch, loveseat, and matching chair were purchased with matching brown plush carpeting. Drapes, kitchen cabinets, bathroom vanities, and all the accessories were decided through my efforts. Graduation day was approaching quickly. We would move into the house the day before. I was overwhelmed.

My heart ached for Marsha, Dee, and Rose. There was no one nearby to play with. Our house that had caught fire was one-half mile away and all our friends lived on that street, but we weren't allowed to venture that far away.

I would try to spend time with them as much as I could. It seemed that we all bonded in front of the old blonde console stereo with the tan speakers built right into the case. When the lid was lifted, there was a turntable for records and a radio. Marsha and I would listen to the Everly Brothers, the Chuck-wagon Gang, Hank Williams, and Peter, Paul, and Mary. Dee and Rose would play nearby. Marsha and I continued to spend hours learning songs and harmonizing just like my Italian uncles.

A few years back, I asked for a guitar for Christmas. My parents were hesitant to buy it for me. They said it was a waste of money and I wouldn't play it. To prove them wrong, I learned all the chords and was playing it within three weeks. This added a new dimension and challenge to our sessions. Music helped us to get through the turmoil of our lives.

When my parents had their malicious fights, no one would be close enough to hear them. My mother would run out with her dreaded butcher knife, hiding, even in the snow, on our large piece of land. It was dark and the woods were creepy. Sometimes, she would stay out there for hours. Occasionally, my dad would go out to find her and they would fight out on our property for hours. All the while, we girls were paralyzed with fear in our beds. I grew to hate that house and everything about it.

I was told college was out of the question because of the purchase of the house and the threat of a possible strike at the steel mill where dad worked. "Why waste money on a girl going to college?" Dad would say. "They just end up married anyway." There went all my dreams down the tube. I looked for a job.

I was hired at a grocery store in the meat department. I actually liked working there. It got me out of that house! Tom, the meat manager was a filthy-minded flirt and made disgusting sexual comments to me. I felt so uncomfortable. Lucy and Marge were two older women who worked in the department and hovered over me like mother hens to protect me from Tom. It was all done in fun, but I still wanted away from Tom.

I moved to a cashier and enjoyed that also, but I looked forward to the end of my shift when I would get back home to Marsha, Dee, and Rose. I worried about their safety all day. We would sing to pass the time. Dee and Rose would chime in with Marsha and I. For a short time, the deadly silence was broken.

MumMum loved to hear us sing and invited Marsha, Dee, Rose, and me to her church for a concert. We sang country, folk, and easy listening music for years, but now we had to learn "religious" music. We were excited and accepted the challenge. Choosing songs and learning them gave us all a purpose. As the oldest at eighteen, I took charge and played my guitar. I taught nine-year old, Dee and three-year old Rose the melody. Marsha, fifteen, sang high harmony and I sang low harmony. It all came together naturally. We practiced long and hard. We couldn't disappoint MumMum. Everyone was pleased with our little concert. This sparked a desire to learn more songs and we spent more quality time together. Life was a little brighter with our music.

When I got home from my job or on my days off, my mother started to ask me to take her shopping while my father was working the evening shift. In return, she made me a deal to let me see my boyfriend for a couple hours. I felt guilty, but we blamed my father's outrageous rules. Soon enough, this plan backfired on me. My mother demanded my services and I took her where she wanted to go. She would stay out almost up to the time I was to leave for my date. I was nervous and upset because I was rushed to get home and to get ready to go. I would dash into the house to shower and dress in time and then she demanded, at the last minute, that I clean the house before I was allowed to go. Her constant manipulation made my life miserable and by the time of my date, I was so sick and upset I didn't even feel like going. When I did go, I dare not be one minute late getting home. Our dates were limited on what we had time to do because of this timetable I was on and the rules of CJ's foster mother. Many nights, we were under so much stress, I cried all night. I didn't know what to do or who or where to turn to. At nineteen years old, I had to sneak to see CJ, worked a fulltime job, and had to be in the house from a date at ten! I had to get in before my father came home from work at eleven fifteen so he would not find out I had a date. One evening, I walked in about ten fifteen and was greeted with a hard sole of a shoe that Mom flung in my face as I opened the door. Over and over, I was struck in my face and head, while being called the filthiest degrading names. My mother pushed me to my breaking point. With a surge of adrenalin, I grabbed her arm in mid-air and through clenched teeth, I notified her she would never, ever strike me again. She knew I meant it. She never hit me again after that incident.

The situation at CJ's foster home was escalating. He saved some money and secretly planned on moving. One morning, when Goldie and Al left for work, he packed up the car and moved into an apartment. I helped him return the car and look for another to get him back and forth to work.

I was sick at my stomach all the time. It was my nerves from all the manipulation and stress of my life. My mother constantly accused me of being pregnant. These accusations were very painful, especially since I had decided on my own to save myself for marriage. I got so tired of hearing I was pregnant that I felt like becoming sexually active. What did it matter anymore?

I couldn't wait to leave that house; I hated my life. I became more and more desperate. Maybe marriage was the way out of my situation. CJ and I had talked about it often. Now that he was on his own with a job, marriage didn't seem so farfetched. The only time we had any peace in our lives was when we were together. We fell in love and bonded over our dysfunctional situations of life. We understood each other's pain.

I decided to take a stand as CJ did. I became more outspoken. I refused to be manipulated anymore. I was twenty. I was tired of being told what I could and could not do. I was an adult and needed to make my own decisions, physically, emo-tionally, and spiritually. I needed to find who I was.

Through the years, I continued to attend church and fulfilled all the requirements to find the favor of God and man. I played my guitar and sang for the folk masses, but my soul became more and more dissatisfied. I felt empty and my spirit cried out wanting more. I ached for love and acceptance. I realized deep down inside that I wasn't the terrible person that my mother said I was, but I needed reassurance from the God who made me and I didn't know how to get that. The more I repeated the prayers I had learned and the more I strived to keep all the laws of the church, the more frustrated I became.

CJ joined me in my God-hunt and we ended up with a group of friends also searching for spiritual truth. We attended home meetings where some of my questions were answered. We attended services and most of our friends were baptized and became a part of this cult-like group. But I recognized a familiar feeling in my spirit, the one that I felt at Mom's. I refused to go back. We continued our search for truth. We had to have a spiritual foundation for our future family.

Our engagement was announced. It was not accepted well by my family, but that was our decision. We were getting married and nobody would change our minds.

Chapter 9

Five Wonderful Blessings

"Children are a heritage from the LORD, offspring a reward from him." Psalm 127:3 (NIV)

Marriage satisfied the deepest desires of my heart. I always dreamt about finding my knight in shining armor. In my dreams, he would sweep me off my feet and carry me away to live happily ever after with a bunch of beautiful, happy children.

I was twenty when I stood arm in arm with my father, ready to walk down the white crash carefully laid on the freshly cut grass of my parent's property. The wooded hillside provided just enough shade in the heat of that muggy July afternoon. The soft breeze filled the air with the sweet fragrance of my bouquet. CJ, my knight, wore a black crushed velvet suit as he waited to put the ring on his fair maiden's trembling hand. Since we wanted God's covering on us, but were not yet part of any church, my grandmother's minister agreed to marry us. It was a beautiful day with beautiful music, our loved ones were present, our hand-written vows were said as a white dove circled above us, and a wonderful time of celebration before we left for our honeymoon to start our life together.

We found a house to rent, situated above a two-car garage with a small kitchen, an undersized living room, a little wee bedroom, and a teeny tiny bathroom. Working to pay off our new furniture was a joint effort. After what seemed like endless payments, we finally experienced a real sense of achievement! Debt free; now I just wanted a baby!

Motherhood is a calling. Some women are perfectly content without children. They have no trouble with the biological clock ticking away, their lives fulfilled with relationships, careers, social events, vacations, and relaxation. Some desire children and they love and care for them, but are committed to other important goals in their life also. On the other hand, there are those who desire children more than anything in this world. They yearn for a child so much that it consumes their thoughts, sometimes for years. This longing of their heart for a little one seems endless until that that day finally arrives when they can say, "I am going to have a baby!" Parenting is their career of choice; nothing else matters. I was one of those women. I was called to motherhood.

Because I was a "mother" to Rose and a protector of Marsha and Dee, I struggled with guilt when I married. Even though I only lived a short distance away, I felt like I abandoned them. Marsha was three years younger than me. She had a spitfire personality and I knew she would be alright. Dee internalized it all and bit her nails to the bone; too much stress for a twelve-year old. My heart broke for her. Rose now was four, just a baby. My concern was beyond words. I planned to get my sisters and take them to my house on my days off. I planned sleepovers. I planned to be available if they needed anything. I planned to visit often.

On my visits, we learned and sang songs for hours. It lightened the weight of the heaviness that existed at the house. We all enjoyed it. MumMum's pastor invited us back to sing. He also went to a minister's convention and gave our information to all his peers. I started to receive calls from different churches for us to come and do a concert. CJ got involved as a narrator and introduced our group and each song with scripture or an inspirational thought. It all happened so fast. We needed a name. We decided since there were four sisters and one husband, we would call ourselves "Four Plus One." That is how God birthed our ministry before we even knew Him. We were searching and He found us! This was a beautiful way that He chose to bond us together, to tolerate awful circumstances, and to draw us to Him.

CJ and I began to talk with my cousin, Luann. She was labeled in our family as the "religious fanatic." I used to avoid her like the plague because of her reputation, but I was getting desperate. Just maybe she could give me the list of things I needed to perform to get in touch with God. Maybe I didn't have the right prayers. Maybe I had missed the boat and what I felt didn't have anything to do with God at all. Maybe I had already experienced my hell on earth and had paid the price for heaven.

We visited my cousin's church. I was overwhelmed with the love and acceptance I found there. I was mesmerized with the preaching from the Bible-the same bible that I used to read at my grandmother's house! *What a coincidence!* But I soon found out that this was no coincidence; it was the divine plan of the Almighty God. This Bible, preached with anointing power, spoke to me about unconditional love and forgiveness, about acceptance, about security, about a plan for my life, and a guarantee of an eternal life with God away from all the tension, pain, stress, and disappointment of this life that we know here on earth. God himself through His Word was meeting me right where I was; broken, unhappy, unloved, insecure, confused, disappointed, and haunted with memories of my past. The God of the Universe was offering me peace, forgiveness, happiness, joy, and security; things that I had never experienced in my life. I wanted that, but I couldn't help but wonder what I had to do to get it. Then I heard the pastor say that it was a free gift to anyone that wanted it and Jesus was waiting, knocking on the door of my heart. God loved me, really loved me, so much that He sacrificed His son Jesus for me. I had never felt love from those who should have loved me and here was Jesus who I didn't even know, expressing His unconditional love for me! He loved me even before I knew Him! And He was the answer I had been searching for all those years! He is the one who is all-knowing, but accepts me for who I am with all my imperfections and loves me anyway. He is offering me value and self-worth. Jesus is the one that is the same yesterday, today, and forever! He offers me peace instead of confusion. Jesus is the one that will never leave me or forsake me. He offers me security. He is the one that is all forgiving. He offers me eternal life with Him in heaven. Jesus is the one who promises to provide for me and to comfort me. He is the answer to all my heart longed for. Jesus is my answer to my wounded, empty heart, to my broken spirit, to my destroyed self-worth, to my devalued and desolated life.

I fell on my knees before Jesus on that Sunday evening at the age of twenty-one and I gave Him my heart, my soul, my fears, my heartache, my insecurities, my pain, and my life. CJ surrendered, too. I prayed, "Dear Jesus, come into my heart and life and live in and through me. Please don't ever leave. Forgive me of any sin I have ever committed. Jesus, please don't let this closeness and peace and love I feel ever go away." Jesus Christ answered that prayer and I have never been the same. Did He erase my past? No. Did my life become free of problems? No. But He is everything I searched for all those years. CJ and I were baptized together. It felt so great to have a clean slate and a brand-new life with Christ!

Psalm 139

Cheryl Marie

Violence and hopelessness;

Longing for some tenderness

And loving arms that say that someone cares.

Just a hug to say good-night;

Assuring words, it will be alright-

It's just a wish because they're never there.

Each day and night, my heart cries out

Just what is life all about?

Don't understand this emptiness I feel

My world is full of fear and doubt
And there seems to be no way out;
There is no love around me that I feel.

Lost, then searching, now I'm found.
Jesus turned my life around;
He answered my desperate, humble plea.

Freedom, joy, and blessed peace,
Blessings that will never cease-
So glad that He came and rescued me.

Everything is different now;
On my face there is a smile
And life is worth the living, I must say.

I've found out what it's all about
And I'm so happy I could shout
Jesus is the truth, the life, the way!

He saw my need and He lifted me
Oh Lord, I thank you, Lord.
From turmoil and strife, He gave me new life

Oh, I'll never turn away from His love.

He turned my wailing into dancing,
He clothed me with His joy
And I will mourn no more, no more.

I cannot keep it quiet, my heart just has to sing
And give Him praise and thanks forever-
My Jesus, my Savior, my King!

I couldn't wait to share the good news with Marsha, Dee, and Rose. They all came to church. They all surrendered their life to Christ. We changed our group's name to "New Beginning." Now we all had something we couldn't wait to sing about!

"You turned my wailing into dancing; you removed my sackcloth and clothed me with joy." Psalm 30:11 (NIV)

I learned that I was pregnant one and one-half years later. That moment was the happiest of my whole life thus far. The world came alive. I became more aware of the beauty around me, the scent of fresh air, the colors of nature, and the tickle of the wind as it blew against my face. "I was having a baby! Thank you, God!" I prayed. I endured the relentless morning sickness and the overwhelming fatigue with a huge satisfying smile on my face. As the months went by, I was getting closer and closer to having my own child.

Then it happened-the sudden gush of bright red blood, the emergency doctor visit, the long days and nights of complete bed rest, and finally, the feared miscarriage that destroyed my world. That death ended all that was alive and beautiful! My heart was crushed. But because I was a child of God, I trusted that He knew best. I stuffed my pain deep down inside my being as I learned to do so well during my lifetime, I told myself to be strong and that I would have the opportunity to have more children. Because CJ didn't talk to me about his pain and didn't want to talk about mine, I felt isolated and alone. I felt like the only survivor on an island after a shipwreck. I never expected to feel this alone being married. That hollow existence of my childhood returned. Even though I mourned my devastating loss, I did find some comfort knowing that I will meet my baby someday in Heaven and will have the wonderful opportunity to share with him or her how much they were loved and how I dreadfully missed having them in my life here on earth.

I was thankful for the job change I had made three years before. It helped to take my mind off the terrible ache in my heart. Working in the busy office enabled me to meet many new people and develop normal friendships. I had never been able to do that growing up. I always felt like I was in a prison, not allowed to have a social life or friends. But since working and getting married, I could experience what life was really like in a world beyond the confines of my tumultuous childhood dwelling.

The supervisor of my department was the main reason that I loved going to work. Besides my grandmother and Aunt Paula, Betty was the most impressive, extraordinary, and remarkable person I had ever met in my whole life. I had never seen anyone smile so much. I had never heard such positivity. I had never seen such helpfulness and kindness to everyone. Even though she was the same age as my mother, she was the complete opposite personality. I was immediately drawn to this inspiring woman and grew to look to her as my other mother. Betty seemed fond of me also. I would seek out a time every day to talk to her about anything other than work. I loved being in her presence and I loved the way she made me feel like a real and valuable person. She and my grandmother were the only people that cared.

All my dreams came true the following year. I was pregnant and I worked until my eighth month with my feet propped up on a stool under my large grey office desk. I was excited and looking forward to the birth of my baby.

But I was troubled and sad because I would not be returning to my job and would not get to see my other mother every day. Her friendship with me was like balm to my wounded spirit. She gave me the spark to be the best person I could be. We made a pact that we would keep in touch and she would remain in my life.

My first child was born, a beautiful little girl, perfect in every way. She was everything I could have ever asked for. Jillian was sweet, talented, smart, and her smile would light up a room and warm the atmosphere as the sun lights up and warms the earth. She was truly my sunshine. She filled a hole in my battered heart.

CJ and I had talked about having our children two years apart. Even though we still had some time, we decided to look for a larger home. Since I was going to be a stay-at-home mom, we couldn't afford much on CJ's meager income. We prayed that God would provide a home we could afford. Because of His faithfulness, we located a small two-story house with affordable rent. I'll never forget our first walkthrough. It had a dirty, musty smell that penetrated my nose, bringing tears to my eyes. The walls were covered with brown stains that looked like coffee had been hurled against them. The carpets were just nasty! The fact that Jillian would have her own room plus a playroom motivated me to agree to move. During the day while CJ was at work, I spent the next three weeks painting every wall in every room upstairs twice and every wall in every room in the downstairs three times to cover the brown stains! I scrubbed, I disinfected, I cleaned, I deodorized! We bought second hand carpets, cleaned them thoroughly, picked up the old carpeting, and covered the floors. Our furniture was moved and we settled into our new home. When I was done with it, it smelled clean and fresh and it looked like a little doll house. I was so happy to have worked so hard to have a larger home to enjoy and to be able to expand my family.

The church we attended was only a few blocks away. We were there every time the doors opened. I craved spiritual knowledge and experiences more than I craved food. We were involved in everything that was happening at our church. CJ was a board member and I was in the choir and on the worship team. Along with my cousin, Luann and her husband, we both also became Children's Ministry leaders. We were part of a huge, supportive, and loving family. God had blessed us!

At two years old, Jillian decided she wanted to sing like Mommy. She had inherited my love for music and she would not be denied the opportunity to use her God-given talents. No, I wouldn't do what my parents did to me. I would be a better parent.

I was working on a concert with a large group of children, helping them to discover the talents and gifts that God had given them. They ranged from six to twelve years of age. They were singers, dancers, poets, and instrumentalists. Jillian announced her decision to sing "We've Got A Great Big Wonderful God" in that children's service. With great determination, she practiced and conquered all the words, the beats, the rests. Even though she sang it perfectly, I wondered what this tiny two-year old would do when she stood on that platform in front of hundreds of faces in a packed sanctuary. Surprisingly, she strutted confidently to her place on the platform, took the large heavy microphone in her pale, white, tiny but chubby hands, and belted out every word to that song right on pitch with a huge grin and a voice bigger than her petite little frame! The standing ovation from the congregation of approximately six hundred fueled her to travel and sing with our family group for years to come. At six, she appeared on Christian TV, flashing that gorgeous smile as she sang her little heart out for Jesus! Mature beyond her years, she was a precious little lady! Finally, a mother! My heart was flooded with adoration. Jillian was a dream come true, my little angel. Kisses and hugs and squeezes could not begin to express my love for her. She brought such joy; I was so happy!

We were blessed with a beautiful, bouncing baby boy when Jillian was two. He was just as perfect, just as sweet, and just as precious. God had showered his goodness on us, not once, but twice!

Scott was not thriving well and was sickly. One evening, I put him to bed at seven thirty. He was fine. A short while later, Scott woke, burning with a one hundred four-point two temperature. This was the way it had been for the last four months. This frail child had suffered almost continuously with a sore throat, rattling chest, labored breathing, and severe skin eczema. His tiny ears were constantly infected and because of the congestion, he couldn't breathe through his cute little button nose. We had to take Scott to the pediatrician at least once every ten days and call him several times in between. No injections, ear drops, or oral medication seemed to help. Instead of gaining, Scott was losing anywhere from a few ounces to two pounds each month. This was critical considering that he was only about sixteen pounds at his heaviest weight. Our son seemed miserable and nothing I could do as his mother could comfort him. The antibiotics would reduce the fever, but suddenly and unexpectedly it would often spike to one hundred four degrees for no apparent reason. Pale and listless, he slept most of the time. The doctor was attributing all of these symptoms to allergies, but Scott was too young to be put through the series of tests to find out what he was allergic to. One day, on one of our emergency visits, the doctor informed me that Scott had every sign of cystic fibrosis and he probably would not grow to be a man. I took my baby boy home and as I tucked him in for his afternoon nap, I collapsed in tears as the reality of my son's diagnosis sank in. Alone and scared, I cried and bargained with God for my little one's life. "No! No! No! Please God, I'll do anything! Just don't let him die!" I begged. My thoughts were racing through my head. *How many more times would I have the privilege of tucking my precious son into his crib for his nap?*

Even though I was a new believer and had surrendered my life to Christ, my faith was strong. I pulled myself together and at four thirty that afternoon, my two children and I drove into town to pick up CJ at work. It was a quiet ride home, but as we arrived, our pastor was sitting on our front porch, waiting to pray with us. It was then that our faith came alive. We claimed victory and we knew our God would pull us through. Family and friends who didn't know the Lord were baffled and concerned about the way we, as a family, were handling ourselves during this time of trouble in our lives.

They said, "Your son is going to die! Why are you acting as though nothing is wrong?"

The doctor arranged for other consultations and tests. A few days later, as we drove Scott to the ear specialist, we asked the Lord for some sign to assure us that Scott was going to be okay. The ear doctor examined Scott's ears and told us that they were swollen shut and it looked as though allergies had caused this condition. Tubes were inserted through his eardrums the following week. We thanked God for victory. We were scheduled for an appointment at Children's Hospital and continued to pray for another sign to stir our faith. As the nurse came to take Scott for his test for cystic fibrosis, her words were from God to us as she said, "I'm not supposed to say this, but he sure doesn't look like a cystic fibrosis child." We praised God once again for giving us sweet assurance that He was at work.

The day arrived for Scott's next check-up with the pediatrician. He had not been sick for over one month, a miracle in itself. After his examination, the doctor sat behind his large, yet fully cluttered wooden desk. His sober expression and his professional mannerisms reminded me of a judge ready to declare a sentence to a convicted felon. CJ and I sat on the edge of our chairs, nervously leaning forward, anticipating his conclusive diagnosis. As he looked into our eyes, he coughed into his large rounded fist, and communicated that Scott had gained some weight and had no sign of any problem with his breathing. His ears and throat were clear and the skin eczema had completely disappeared. With a smile on his face, the doctor beamed and his words were to us were, "Scott is going to grow to be a man!" Praise the Lord!

God did a miracle and saved Scott's life. It was an answer to our prayers. He developed a whole new, glowing complexion. In the span of a few weeks, blonde ringlets replaced his straight brown hair. He didn't sleep most of the day. He gobbled his food instead of clamping his mouth shut. A happy personality emerged. His sad eyes twinkled. Scott looked like a totally different child. My listless, inactive son became a little powerhouse that never ran out of energy! He was so full of life that we used to wonder if, when God healed him, He gave him a double dose of energy because He always gives us more than we ask for.

When he was about three and one-half, we had three visits to the emergency room in a three-week span. One warm summer day, he was on his little riding toy on the sidewalk in front of our house. The wheel hit a large crack and tossed both Scott and his riding toy forward. In a split second, he was face down in a pool of blood. His two front teeth were literally hanging from his purple swollen gums. He was admitted to the hospital to surgically remove his two front baby teeth. As a result, he was missing those two front teeth until he was seven. A few weeks later, we were in a store and Scott wanted to ride on the bottom of the cart. Fascinated with the rotation, he put his fingers under the wheel and smashed them. I thought they were broken. Another trip to the hospital. Again, in a department store a short time later, I turned my back for a second. He decided to climb a shelf to see a toy that was out of his reach, slipped and fell backward and hit his head, knocking himself out. In the emergency room for the third time in three weeks, I faced suspecting looks, questioning glares, and accusing interrogations! As you can understand, I would describe Scott as spunky, a handful, full of energy, but as cute as a button.

My pastor and church family had witnessed Scott's healing and transformation. Our family group was traveling and holding services at different churches and we always testified of the great things that the Lord was doing in our lives. I told of Scott's healing. Word of his miracle spread and we were invited to share Scott's testimony on Channel 40 Christian TV. We shared how, after prayer, all his symptoms disappeared permanently. Our family group, including Jillian, was also invited to sing. I had also shared a song I wrote about Scott's healing. My hope was to encourage others to believe God for their healing.

The duties and joyous sounds of children at play filled my days and my nights. A handsome little boy and a charming little girl were the answers to my happiest dreams and deepest desires. I couldn't believe that I had more than enough love for two children! I was so blessed to have them in my world. My life revolved around my two little sweethearts. I tried to give them all the unconditional love and spiritual guidance that I could. CJ and I took our family to church when the doors were open and the children were introduced to Jesus while they were very young. I taught them to sing all their Sunday School songs. They slept on the church pews at least two evenings a week. I thrived on caring for them and protecting them. I loved their big inquisitive eyes, their little arms around my neck, their innocent conversations, the sweet scent of their soft skin. Flooding both of them with affection, I tried with everything in me to be the best, the kindest, the most loving mom that I could.

This was extremely important to me. My childhood was filled with memories that I just wanted to forget, but instead I relived them in my mind every day and in my dreams every night. I had never told anyone about it. I kept every detail locked within me like a vault without a key or combination. I still had so much pain stuffed within my being.

Adjusting to live on a tight budget was one of the biggest challenges of my young life. I learned to sew many of my children's clothes and used wisdom on all essential purchases. Cutting coupons was not my favorite pastime, but was neces-sary. Every gift-giving holiday, I spent months planning and making homemade presents for our families. We were making it.

My parents continued to involve me in their dysfunction. My mom would call me, while they were fighting, crying and spilling out her side of the story while my dad would be in the background protesting. Mom would beg me to come down to the house to intervene. There were times when they drove up to my house and fought in my backyard in earshot of all my neighbors. I turned up the TV or put on music. One time, they brought their fight through my opened back door into my kitchen. They screamed and cursed, and called each other names in front of my startled children. I had had enough! I yelled above their screams, "How dare you come into my house with your stupid fighting! You have done this to me my whole life and I will not allow you to do this to my children. They have never heard a bad word. Don't you ever use a curse word in front of me or my children ever again! Get out of my house! Now! Get out! Get out!" My parents left immediately. I'm sure I shocked them when I said what I did. I was so angry! How dare they shatter the peacefulness of my loving home! I didn't know how I could take any more.

I called Betty and asked if we could talk. I needed to vent to a non-judgmental and understanding person. I didn't expect her to fix anything. My grandmother couldn't and neither could my aunts and uncles. I needed a listening ear, someone older with life experience and wisdom. She was the only person outside my family that I felt safe enough to talk to. I knew she wouldn't judge me or walk away. For the first time in my life, I spilled out the raw, gory details like I had thrown up after food poisoning. She was dumbfounded with my story and amazed at the person I was in spite of my background. Her compassion, understanding, support, and love for me made me feel like I was not alone in my daily struggles. She was just a phone call away.

Now, I had to let go, move on, put the past behind me, and continue to focus on doing the best for my little family. CJ and I considered moving away. We'd pray about it.

My parents were careful, after the incidence at my home, with their language in front of my family. The only time I saw them was when I came to practice music with my sisters.

We met at Mom and Dad's house. We purchased a keyboard, drums, a bass guitar, and a small PA system. Marsha taught herself to play bass guitar. Rose taught herself keyboard and drums. I played guitar. We gave Dee a tambourine and teased her that she must have been adopted. All this was set up in the basement of my parent's home. The girls and I would go straight downstairs and stay there the whole evening. We spent very little time with either of my parents. Jillian joined our group and loved being with us. CJ stayed at home with Scott during our practices and when we traveled to churches. For twelve years, God opened doors for us to share Jesus. It was wonderful to see how God used this broken family.

I was ill for weeks with a low-grade fever, fatigue, and an upset stomach. I was diagnosed with a virus. A short time later, I experienced morning sickness and some physical changes in my body that caused me to suspect that I was pregnant. I went to the doctor and he ran some tests that were inconclusive. I returned home, frustrated, with no relief. Certain that I was pregnant, I returned to his office and the doctor ordered a sonogram. The results were disheartening. He explained that a double sac had detached itself from my uterus. He believed that the babies had already died and the decay was poisoning me. The doctor made arrangements for my admittance to the hospital that very day to remove my twins from my body. I was heartbroken again.

I didn't know what to do with the pain. I cried when no one was around and put on a brave face in the presence of others. Even though our loss had to hurt him, CJ went on with life seemingly unaffected and offered me no comfort. His lack of compassion was devastating and another blow to our marriage. Doing what I had always done, I stuffed all the disappointment down deep inside, like one would shove garbage deep down to the bottom of a full trash can. I proclaimed what every good Christian should say. "It was God's will and He knows best." I remained very close to Betty, but even sharing with her did not lessen my pain. I was struggling, but acted like I was fine, I hid my tears and pretended that it didn't hurt; pretended that I was strong and could move on. After all, I was an expert at this.

Having miscarried three babies within such a short period of time made it difficult for me to put a smile on my face and to act like everything was hunky dory. I felt so isolated and detached from everyone. I was living in a foggy dream. At times when I was alone, I would cry out to God. "Why all the pain? Haven't I suffered enough?" I sobbed. I was in my twenties and could barely count, on one hand, the times I had a wonderful memory about something in my life. I realized that I had a tremendous amount of disappointment and anger buried deep inside from as far back as my childhood. I had a difficult time expressing my feelings. I learned to conceal them well. *Was I angry at God? If not, who?* I really didn't know. I think I was just plain old angry. I endured such agonizing heartbreak my whole life. All that had happened made the terrible pain feel like it had been stuffed in my torso and now was overflowing and seeping into every limb. I cried out, "Lord, what do I do with all the heartache and disappointment?" Struggling to hold back the flood of tears as best as I could, I threw myself into the care of my children and home. It was a hard, stressful, and challenging time in my life. My song, "Does He Really Care" came from the depths of my anguish.

Does He Really Care?

Cheryl Marie

There are those times when life's a struggle
And my burdens are hard to bear.
I feel alone, though He's always with me.
And I ask myself, does He really care?

I'm feeling tired and I'm feeling hopeless.
Disappointment fills the air.
I try to pray but I hear no answers
And I ask myself, does He really care?

The Bible says that His love's amazing,
It stretches to the heavens above,
It's deeper than the deepest ocean;
I will rest in God's great love.

He knows my need, He hears my cry,
To bear such pain, sometimes I feel like dying.
He knows where I am and He sees my hurting heart.
I will wait on you, Lord, your peace you will impart.

I must stand strong and I must trust;
I must not question His love so rare.
I know He's working His plan for me.
In faith, I do believe, that He really cares.

CJ didn't make a lot of money and we were in a serious financial bind. In spite of my terrible home life as a child, my parents always provided well for us with food and clothing. They were there for us in our current crisis, helping in many ways with necessities for the children. We were privileged to be part of a wonderful, loving, and powerful church group who were standing with us in prayer and ready to help us in any way they could.

One evening, we received an unexpected and disturbing phone call. The deep manly voice said "Go out to your front porch. There is something for you." I became very alarmed and my imagination took me to situations that I had witnessed in scary movies I had seen. *Who was the man? Why did he call us? What would happen when we opened our front door?* I thought. CJ cautiously pulled back the door and in the blackness of that clear, moonlit night, we saw on our porch, a huge and bulky TV box. This was not like our modern, slender TVs of today. This box was one that held an old-time console TV and was large enough to hold a person in a kneeling position. Feelings of fear and apprehension were amplified among all of us. "What should we do?" I asked CJ. My children's eyes were as big as saucers. Even though it was a mild night, I was trembling and shivering like I was outside in freezing weather without a coat. CJ cautiously approached the box, stood staring at it, and then his curiosity got the best of him. Flipping open the one side flap of the lid, he quickly backed himself inside the house and waited. Nobody jumped out so he guardedly went onto the porch one more time, flipped open the other side flap of the lid, and backed into the house so fast that he nearly knocked me over. Nothing bad or scary happened. Feeling safe, CJ took a look inside and it was filled with food, so much that we couldn't even drag the box into the house. Everybody helped as we carried meat, vegetables, fruit, and canned goods into the house and filled the refrigerator and cupboards! What a blessing in our time of need!

"And my God will meet all your needs according to the riches of his glory in Christ Jesus." Philippians 4:19 (NIV)

When the children asked who gave us the food, CJ and I had the opportunity to share the provision of God to them. They will always remember the day when the angels delivered the food to our door! How wonderful it is when we allow God to work through us to bless others. We thanked God for whoever supplied that food that night. Their obedience to Him made an impact on all of us!

"I was young and now I am old, yet I have never seen the righteous forsaken or their children begging bread." *Psalm 37:25 (NIV)*

Dee ran away from home at sixteen. She married her boyfriend and they moved into an apartment a few miles away. She wasn't pregnant. She moved to get out of the atmosphere of my parent's house. Marsha married four months later and moved out. Rose was left alone with my parents with no one to protect her. How I worried.

I went to Children and Youth Services and explained Rose's living conditions. I told of the mental, emotional, and physical abuse. I begged to have her removed from the home. I offered to be her guardian. She could live with me. I would do anything I had to do to save her. "Because there are no hospital records or police reports filed to show bodily injury or death, we can't help you," the lady said. I stood in shock. "Really? You can't be serious! Is this how you protect innocent children? What am I supposed to do? I can't sit back and wait until Rose is dead!" I sobbed. "If you go ahead and take her anyway, you will be charged with kidnapping," she warned. I couldn't believe my ears. I was angry, disappointed, frustrated, and heartbroken. My hands were tied. I needed God's help to get through all this.

Betty continued to be my confidant and support and became Aunt Betty to my children, who all adored this special lady. We spent many summer evenings with her at the playground near her house where the children played as we sat and caught up on everything that had happened since the last time we spoke. On other visits, she and her husband, Jim enjoyed spending time with my babies, since they had never had children of their own. I'm sure my children and their funny antics filled an empty hole in their hearts just like their presence did in mine. Jim became a man that I admired and would run to for advice. He never forced me to see things his way or rejected me like my dad did. I admired and loved them both. Those precious memories I will forever hold dear to my heart.

CJ was dismissed from his job due to cutbacks. I was expecting our third child. Not a good time to lose our health coverage! I had a wonderful doctor for my first two children, a kind and compassionate Jewish man. After my second visit, I informed him that I would be transferring to the medical clinic because we no longer had our health insurance. He put his arm around my shoulder and pulled me close as a father would do. "I will not hear of you going to the clinic. I delivered both your babies and I'm delivering this one, too. Don't you worry about paying me or the hospital. You concentrate on having a healthy baby and let me worry about everything else," he said as he gave me a gentle squeeze. I could continue to carry my baby without financial stress. What a blessing!

I wished the burden of my parent's relationship was removed like the financial stress, but that continued. We had a joint birthday party every year for Jillian and Scott since they were born in the month of August two years apart. We always invited Mom and Dad, all my sisters and their families, my aunt and uncle, MumMum, and my grandfather. I called everyone to come. My father told me that he would not come unless my mother and grandparents were uninvited. I stood my ground and told him boldly that the invitation was for everyone, as it has always been, and I hoped that he would come. He stubbornly stated that he "was done with me" if I would not do what he asked. Upset, I hung up the phone and decided that I had to do what was right. I was so hurt, but I would not tell people in my family they couldn't attend my children's party. Dad never showed. He was "done with me" again.

I carried Brock, my third child, three weeks past my delivery date. I was in distressing labor intermittently during this span of time, but was sent home from the hospital several times with the assurance that the baby would come when it was time. After the third week, I was experiencing stronger, more deliberate pain and it was discovered that the cord had been wrapped around my baby boy's neck and each time my child began to move down the birth canal, the cord tightened and stopped the progress. After a grueling labor, my very large baby boy was born with a warning that the cord could have caused brain damage. Again, I put my trust in the Lord's hands and begged Him to give me a healthy child and that He did! Brock was a beautiful, blonde haired, blue eyed boy! Because I was three weeks overdue, He was eight pounds fifteen ounces. This was considerably larger than Jillian and Scott. I was elated to have another child to love.

I was never charged a cent for all the office visits for the term of my pregnancy, any tests administered, my delivery, or my hospital stay. What a blessing my doctor was! God used this man to help us in our time of need.

"Because of the LORD's great love, we are not consumed, for his compassions never fail. They are new every morning; great is your faithfulness." Lamentations 3:22, 23 (NIV)

Rose was withdrawn and her grades were plummeting. I was worried about her. One afternoon, Marsha and Rose were at my parent's home. The fights between my parents had escalated and that day, they were having a raging war. It was their last battle because my dad packed up his belongings and left. Because my sisters stood, speechless, and watched dad move out, he assumed they took my mother's side. Dad was "done with them" for decades. I will never understand how my father could throw away, like a piece of trash, his own flesh and blood.

Rose moved in with Dee and soon enough, my mother moved in also. I worried about my sisters. I called Mom often and made small talk just to make sure everyone was doing ok. She seemed different; more relaxed, civil, talkative, even kind. I felt sad for all she'd been through, but I could sense she was more at peace.

CJ had been sending out applications for months. We considered job offers within one hundred miles from where we lived. We would be far enough away to live our life but close enough if there was an emergency. I didn't really want to leave Marsha, Dee, and Rose. I didn't want to move away from my friends, my relatives, MumMum, Betty, my church and my church family, or my ministry with my sisters. I knew we had to go, but I was so torn. I had had no contact with my dad since the birthday party two years ago. He didn't even acknowledge his new grandson's birth. When we announced our move to Mom, she carried on and cried, "Please don't move and take your kids away from me. How could you do this to me?" I wanted to say, *"It is all yours and Dad's fault that we are moving. Stop putting a guilt trip on me! I am sacrificing all my good relationships just so I can get away from you both!"* Instead, I walked away.

We left our house in a busy neighborhood in the city and moved to a quiet Amish town of fifty families. I settled into country living. I loved the fresh air, no longer breathing in the pollution of city life. I loved the chirping birds instead of the noise of our former neighborhood. I loved the clomping sound of horse's hooves on the pavement as they pulled their buggies past our house instead of screeching tires and honking horns of strange cars delivering drugs to our neighbors. I loved our acre of property covered with a carpet of lush green grass instead of the small, weedy fenced in yard where we used to live. I loved the peacefulness of this safe and serene community of dairy farms, goats, and chickens instead of the fear of finding a body on the pavement in front of the local bar on the block. We were two and one-half hours away from anyone we knew. We were twenty minutes from the closest town. Our post office was a small coal shed.

It wasn't all easy. Jillian and Scott faced some adjustment challenges at school. Scott came home with a bloody nose after he was punched on the bus. Jillian was teased to tears because she liked to dress up for school. They were the "outsiders" in the community and the local kids made their life difficult. I was thankful they had made a few friends and hoped everything would settle down. CJ took our only car to work every day and I was "stranded" with no transportation. The people in my town were all related and had lived there all their lives. Only a few were friendly towards me so I stayed to myself. I was feeling lonely. I missed my sisters. I missed Betty. I missed my church family. I was depressed about the alienation from my dad. I was so involved in taking care of my children and doing all I had to do at home that I had no time to make friends. CJ was distant and uninvolved. I was disappointed that our marriage wasn't fulfilling. Because of my children, I continued to go on. The passing of time and my busyness helped to lessen the severity of my sadness.

I stayed in touch with Mom daily. She was doing better, but the damage of the dysfunctional relationship was evident. She was introverted because of her isolation with people. She lacked social skills, but had taken a part-time job at a thrift store. This was the first job she ever had since she married my dad and it gave her a reason to get up in the morning. She made friendships. She thrived on purchasing all the new items for my children. I invited her up to our new house for a weekend or a few days during the week. She looked forward to these mini vacations and came with her arms full of bags of surprises. Jillian, Scott, and Brock anticipated her visits. We enjoyed our time with her and she left with fresh fruits and vegetables and gallons of fresh milk from the cows at the local dairy farm.

My estranged relationship with Dad bothered me all the time. I heard nothing from him. I wasn't going to apologize. I did nothing wrong! He did this to me all my life. Every time he gave me the "silent treatment," I begged forgiveness for my unknown failure. I could never figure out what I did to deserve such treatment. I did what he wanted to keep peace. This time was different. For once, I knew exactly what he was upset about. I wouldn't tell Mom, MumMum, and my grandfather they were uninvited. *Sorry Dad, but I stood up to you this time. I did what was right. I did not allow you to manipulate me. You will never receive an apology for this!* I thought. I was upset and depressed about the whole situation, but I would not back down. Even if I never saw him again, I would not give in to his demands. I was an adult and I would stand firm. I had had enough manipulation.

The morning of the second Thanksgiving after we moved away, there was a knock on our door. CJ answered it and there stood my father with a suitcase. I couldn't believe it! He hadn't seen Jillian and Scott for several years. He had never seen Brock, who was eleven months old. Dad came in, made himself at home, and acted like nothing had ever happened. This was hard to understand. Grudges were a way of life for him. He stayed a few days, played with the kids, and returned to his home with no discussion about the day of the party. Puzzled, I wondered what had caused him to come since he proclaimed that he was "done with me."

Brock was growing; he was such a handsome little guy with a vibrant personality and disposition that is rarely seen in one so young. Even as a tot, he had a magnetism that captivated the attention of every adult near him. When he was eighteen months old, he and I were in a doctor's office. Across from us sat a middle-aged, very distinguished looking priest dressed meticulously in his white collar and a black suit. After staring for a short time, my boy squirmed to release my detaining grip and bolted off in the direction of this man. Brock approached him with determination as on a mission, babbling his barely understandable greetings. While toddling with his unbalanced gait, and making focused eye contact, my little guy went tumbling on this minister's spit-shined black wing tipped shoes, all while grabbing the perfectly pressed pant legs of his shiny black suit with stubby, saliva covered fingers. As Brock looked up and focused his attention on the priest's big accepting smile, he proceeded to crawl up on the already damp extended leg and snuggled on the lap of this man of God. My son was drawn to the bright white collar peeping from beneath the priest's matching black shirt and was inspecting it with his chubby, dimpled little hands. Brock then discovered the inside pockets of the suit jacket and there he discovered a small black comb. As I sat there watching this beautiful interaction between my little angel and well-dressed reverend, I couldn't believe my eyes when Brock began to run the teeth of that comb through this man's thick, wavy, grey streaked black locks. I quickly apologized and came to the priest's rescue, but he said with a wide admiring grin, "It's ok, let him be. I have never seen a child who is so open and can relate to adults at such a young age. He has a very special gift. Don't ever squelch what he has. It is beautiful." A while later, when it was time to see the doctor, Brock sweetly planted a kiss on the stranger's cheek in turn for a big squeeze that he abruptly squiggled from and ran away. Shortly after, we attended a wedding of one of my cousins. There in the middle of the crowded dance floor was Brock bopping, wiggling, shaking, and singing in his little navy shorts, navy knee socks, white shoes, white shirt, plaid vest and navy bow tie. His soft blonde curls bounced to the beat as more than one hundred people gathered around him laughing, clapping, and edging him on in his antics. Big blue eyes with long curled lashes and his head of shiny, silky, blonde curls melted my heart and the heart of everyone he knew. He was so sweet and handsome and he brought an additional measure of joy to my life. I kept very busy with my three beautiful children and I loved caring for them.

We found a church and I became the worship leader. Jillian and I accepted invitations to sing at churches and events. Scott joined us on a few occasions.

We were having a difficult time paying all the bills. Since we were short over four hundred dollars each month, we had to do something! CJ invited a man to come to the house to discuss a part-time sales position. After explaining the job to us and listening to our conversation, the man announced that he thought I should sell his product. When he left, CJ and I talked it over and I said I would try it. He promised to care for the children while I worked three to four evenings a week.

I studied the product details, prepared a plan, and set a goal for my sales each week. Each evening that I planned to work, I had a busier than usual day trying to get all my chores done. I had a full-course dinner hot and on the table when CJ walked in the door from work. I ate with my family, kissed them all good-bye and off I went to sell. I asked the Lord to guide me to the people He wanted me to see. I knocked on doors and prayed to talk to potential buyers. Once in the door of their home, I showed them my product and told them about Jesus. I did well and made the needed money, but was even more excited about sharing my faith. I became an area manager two months later. God made a way once again.

I became more disappointed, frustrated, and angry as the months passed. On the evenings I worked, I came home to a mess. Dinner dishes would still be on the table, toys were scattered through the house, and children weren't bathed. CJ always had an excuse.

The all too familiar nausea and fatigue returned. *Could it be another pregnancy?* A visit to my new doctor confirmed my suspicions, but to my surprise, I was carrying twins again! *What did I ever do to deserve His wonderful blessings?*

As apprehension creeped in, I begged the Lord for healthy babies and a safe delivery. I didn't feel like I could bear the heartache of losing another child.

As the term slowly progressed, I found myself able to do less and less. I quit my sales job. CJ needed to do what he had to do to supply the needed money. Severe nausea, general malaise, fatigue, lack of motivation to even get out of bed, pain, and even depression seemed to overtake my will for life to go on and be "normal." Fear and concern became my constant companions. I worried about the outcome of my pregnancy. I was anxious about the condition of my babies. The enemy tortured me with the possibility of miscarriage again. Maybe they would be Siamese twins. Possibly they would come prematurely. Perhaps they would suffer disfigurement or have a severe mental or physical impairment. The more disabled I became, the more obsessed I was about the health of my babies. My poor health caused many negative thoughts.

I spent my days on the couch snuggling and reading books to two-year old, Brock, while Jillian and Scott were at school. I didn't want to deny him the attention he so deserved. Because I was unable to take care of my home and my children to my satisfaction, I carried a lot of guilt. I had met many people through church and school activities, but no one that I could call a close friend. I continued to call Betty often, but she was one hundred miles away. I longed to see her and spend time with her, but I was unable to travel. I felt helpless and alone and I didn't know what to do.

It wasn't long before my mother suggested that she come and stay with us to help with the household chores and to care for the children. Since the separation from my father, she was different. She was released from the "prison" that my dad had locked her in all their married life. Now free, she volunteered to come to my rescue and even after all that had happened between us, I was willing to consider her offer. I was still questioning myself. *Had I really totally forgiven her? I had asked Jesus to help me, but why was I still having nightmares and why the tears when thoughts of my childhood passed through the recesses of my mind? Why was I still asking God to change me when I found myself acting in a way that reminded me of her past behavior? Why the flashbacks? Why did the awful memories linger? What do I do with the pain?*

In addition to not feeling well, I gained seventy pounds very quickly and my belly had grown grossly huge. The back pain was unbearable and I was confined to a wheelchair. I had never received much help from CJ and I didn't expect that to change. I could barely take care of myself. *How could I care for my children, the house, the meals, the laundry, groceries?*

I prayed and decided that I needed to be willing to accept my mother's help. I needed some serious assistance and God had made help available. My mother! Because of our past history, I was worried. *Would I be mentally able to tolerate her presence in my home for a long period of time or her attending to my children?* I couldn't forget how she treated me and my sisters. *How will she treat my babies?* I wondered. She seems different now, I reasoned. I thanked God for my mother's unselfish offer. I have seen both my parents help people a lot over the years. I knew that they both had soft hearts when it came to people in need. Coming to my aid was possibly her chance to be the mother she had failed to be; her opportunity to replace all the bad words and actions with good. I had to give her that chance.

I found myself in the familiar delivery room four miserable months later. The antiseptic aroma filled the brightly lit sterile interior. The clanging of the metal instruments striking each other in preparation for the grand entrance of my children amplified my feelings of nervousness, fear, and anticipation. Carrying the twins over the last thirty-two weeks had taken its toll on my small frame and I was powerless to contain them inside the confines of my womb any longer! The two babies battled for eleven hours over who was coming into this world first!

After the exhausting labor and the very grueling delivery of the first twin, I was totally spent. Shana came out wailing as the nurses quickly took her away. There was no time for bonding when another baby was waiting in the corridor. As I laid on the hard table, I opened my eyes to see the glaring lights and the eyes of several doctors and nurses standing on each side and at the foot of my table. I felt like I was drifting in and out between reality and a dream as I heard the repeated echo of my name and warnings that I had to push to deliver the second baby. I could muster no energy to respond as they frantically begged me to push. I heard my doctor tell the anesthesiologist to get ready and that they would have to do a cesarean to save the baby. CJ, who was seated near my right shoulder, leaned over in front of my face and said, "CHERYL, WE'RE GONNA LOSE THE BABY IF YOU DON'T PUSH!" This abruptly snapped me back to the reality of the pain and anguish of my past miscarriages and the deep love for my existing children. I found the energy for one last push and I heard the cries of my second baby as delirium overtook me. Thinking it was over, I learned that the placenta was still inside me and truthfully, I don't remember the details of how that was removed, only the fact that the placentas of both babies were fused together and weighed nine pounds. Shana weighed four pounds and one ounce and Sheila weighed three pounds and ten ounces. Even though the sum of the babies' total weight was a whopping seven pounds and eleven ounces, the additional nine-pound placenta totaled sixteen pounds and eleven ounces in my belly! No wonder my back hurt and I was in a wheelchair! I felt like my body had been through a raging war.

I brought into this world two beautiful, tiny identical twin baby girls. They weren't Siamese. They weren't disfigured! I was so relieved! How I had allowed the enemy to lie to me, but God was faithful! I was so grateful to Him for His goodness once again.

It took two days before I could even sit up enough to be wheeled down the hall to visit my little girls in the neonatal unit. After five days in the hospital, I still was unable to walk. I went home in a wheelchair. Thank God that Mom was still there to help.

With much prayer, Sheila and Shana's frail little bodies developed well with the care they received in the neonatal unit. Since she was the larger twin, Shana won the battle to be born first. Surprisingly, she was jaundice and had stopped breathing thirty-five times in twenty-four hours. Sheila was tiny, feisty, and under-developed. Shana was placed in the first incubator closest to the entry door in the unit and Sheila was in the last incubator furthest from the door. Shana was very placid and didn't seem to react to my voice. Sheila, on the other hand, would scream at the top of her little lungs as soon as she heard me enter and would not stop until she felt my touch on her frail tiny body. At six weeks of age weighing just five pounds and wearing preemie diapers and clothes, Sheila and Shana finally came home to complete our family. They were healthy, thriving, and absolutely beautiful! Happy day at our house!

I was so thankful that Mom came to stay. She arrived in my third month of pregnancy and made life a whole lot easier. She couldn't have done a better job. She cooked, cleaned, did laundry, and bathed children. I helped as much as I could from a wheelchair. Having her there gave me an opportunity to heal after the birth of the twins and she was a great help when we brought the girls home.

We actually had normal conversations, but we never talked about anything that happened in my childhood. It was probably as painful for her as it was for me. When she left six months later to go back to Dee's house, I missed her. Mom was at her best when she was helping others. We had begun the restoration of our relationship.

What a challenge! A twelve-year old, a ten-year old, a two-year old, and twins! Brock, who had been potty trained for the last six months, decided that he would regress and wore diapers for the next two years until the twins were potty trained! He was then four! I thought he would go to school in diapers! If I left the house, I had three babies, two diaper bags, and two heart monitors, since the twins were attached to them for six months. You can understand why I was content to be home most of the time! Jillian stepped in and became the second mommy and what a blessing she was! I would watch the clock and count the minutes until she would walk in the door from school. I was alone all day with three babies; Relief at last! Finally, I could enjoy a quick shower, get out of my PJ's, get a bite to eat! I couldn't have survived without her help! Her friend and she, on occasion, would take the twins and dress them up in preemie "Cabbage Patch" clothes. One time we were presented with two little five-pound baby girls dressed as Rambo, complete with bandanas!

Each of my five children was the greatest blessing I could ever receive. With each birth I was overwhelmed with emotion. I found motherhood to be the sustaining element to want to go on. I loved my children with a love that I never had, I adored each of them with every fiber of my being. I can't help but anticipate with excitement, the reunion we will have as we gather in Heaven with the precious babies, brothers, sisters, sons, or daughters we were unable to meet and enjoy here on earth.

Chapter 10

Disappointment and Disillusionment

Marriage was a challenge from the start. There we were, two young kids, each from a highly dysfunctional family, desiring and expecting to find marital bliss. Instead, we had much pain. CJ and I each brought so much baggage from our childhood that we were doomed from the start. Former dysfunction in both of our homes set us up for failure.

We dated for three and one-half years. Our time together was hardly ever conducive to the development of our relationship. Instead, our conversations were about trying to figure out and resolve the disastrous situations of our family setting. I'm sure we loved each other, but our love was distorted. Neither of us had the background to even know what real love was.

Growing up as the oldest of four girls, I desired to be a good example to my siblings. Because I carried an enormous amount of misplaced responsibility, caring in many ways for my whole family, I became an experienced caretaker and peacemaker.

Growing up with an absent alcoholic father, CJ lacked the influence of a good male role model. The heartbreaking separation of he and his six-year old sister and placement in the foster care system was very traumatic and affected him greatly. He had to take responsibility for so much as a child, he refused to take it as an adult. It was his season to relax and that he did. I didn't care that I was forced to carry the liability for just about everything. Naive and oblivious to the healthy roles of husband and wife, I accepted my role without dispute, since I had done it all my life. I see now that he was looking to me to be the mother that he had lost.

We had a difficult time adjusting to married life. Because of my upbringing, I had no concept of what a normal relationship should be like. I fell in love and married. All I wanted was out of my house and to start my own family. I would be happy then, I was sure. I had expectations of marriage and became disappointed and frustrated when those expectations were not fulfilled. In hindsight, I see that I was looking to my husband to heal all my past wounds as only Jesus is able.

CJ's expectations of our marriage did not involve our "personal" relationship. He voiced to me that a good wife was one who kept an immaculate house, had meals on the table when her husband got home from work, and took all responsibility for everything involving the kids. Being the caretaker that I had grown to be, his expectations drove me to be more of a perfectionist that I already was.

I became so obsessed with "being a good wife" and earning his love and approval that I lost myself as a person. Becoming a performing robot, I sought appreciation and acceptance that I never received. My house was always spotless. I did all the cleaning, decorating, wallpapering, painting, baking, mending, gardening, and yard work. The laundry was always done, his shirts were dipped in liquid starch, and ironed to perfection. I prepared daily, a full course meal that was hot and waiting on the table every evening when he walked through the door. After bellies were full and little hands and faces were wiped, I cleared the table, put the food away, washed and dried the dishes, and packed the school lunches before trudging up the stairs for bath time, PJs, bedtime stories, prayers, and bed. The house was not only spotless, but in order and the children were taken care of to the best of my ability. They were guided and disciplined, clean and well-dressed at all times. I helped with homework and attended all school functions. My needs were of no importance. I lived to meet my family's needs. Obsessed with being "Super Wife and Mommy," I had no time for myself or to have friendships. I was lonely; I felt like a slave; All I did was give and give and then give some more with no gratitude because that was my job, I signed up for it, and that was expected of me.

I needed a husband's love, support, and understanding. I wanted a partner, a helper, a friend, someone who would share parental responsibility with me after being with five children all day! CJ had a fulltime job at a bank and he took care of our finances. All other responsibilities of the household fell on my shoulders. I felt so tired, so alone, and so frustrated. My days were exhausting and nights were not any better even though I tried to be wise in the timing of the breast feedings. Shana woke first and when she was done, I woke Sheila and fed her. Both were very slow eaters. Usually by the time I had accomplished the task of feeding both twins and coaxing Brock back to sleep, having been awakened by one or sometimes both of the them, Shana woke again for her next feeding and the routine would repeat all over again. I was running on empty and again cried out to God. "I can't do this much longer. Lord. help me. I need strength to go on. Life is really hard right now. I am beyond tired, Lord. I am exhausted." When my smallest munchkins were nineteen months old, I suffered a physical collapse and was ordered by the doctor to at least eight hours of uninterrupted sleep each night for the next six months. No longer could I breastfeed my babies. No longer did I get out of bed to console Brock. CJ had to step up to the plate and take care of the children at night for I did not have any strength left to do so.

"So do not fear, for I am with you; do not be dismayed, for I am your God. I will strengthen you and help you; I will uphold you with my righteous right hand." Isaiah 41:10 (NIV)

CJ and I were drifting further apart. He was content allowing me to take care of all the needs of the children. I asked for him to at least help me with the discipline, but he chose to pass and be the good guy. I needed him to help with some of the chores that were weighing me down, but that was my job. I tried so many times to have meaningful conversations, but he didn't want to be bothered. I pleaded for him to become actively involved in our family, but he wasn't interested in doing so. I longed for CJ to tell me that he liked my cooking or was proud of me for keeping our home so clean and neat, but he didn't. I worked very hard all day to get everything done because I wanted to spend time together as a couple in the evening after the children were put to bed, but he had no desire to do that. The mental, emotional, and physical desertion broke my heart and I spent many nights alone and crying.

Faithfully, CJ, myself, and all the children attended Sunday School, church, and special services. I remember that those were the times I felt like a family, united with a purpose and that was to grow closer to Jesus Christ.

At home, I always felt like we were on totally different pages. There were many happy times and lots of good memories, but serious problems and situations arose that ruined my respect and trust; therefore, most of the marriage was a struggle.

I'm sure CJ felt disappointed also, but I was the one who voiced my dissatisfaction when resolutions were not discussed. Having a very passive personality, he swept our problems under the rug instead of acknowledging them. Because I grew up in an atmosphere of anger, fighting, and violence and nothing was discussed, I wanted to expose our issues, talk them over, and resolve them, if possible. CJ refused to acknowledge any difficulty and even accused me for "creating a dilemma" or "making a mountain out of a molehill" in our marriage. I had no choice but to try to keep peace by continuing to stuff the hurt because I didn't want to create a hostile environment for my children like my parents did. I wanted a good relationship. I wanted to feel loved and appreciated. I can't speak for CJ because he never expressed how he felt, but I desperately desired to be united. I wanted a stable family, but it seemed to be impossible with the path we were on. My hope, my prayer, was to at least have the same goal of saving the marriage for our sakes and the sakes of our children.

Counseling didn't help. I wanted to go and he didn't. Finally, CJ reluctantly attended, but denied that we had a problem and laughed about my concerns while I cried and poured out my heart.

Because he did not take our situation seriously, the sessions left me angry, hurt and frustrated. He refused to follow the counselor's advice and guidance. It was obvious that we would never see eye to eye on anything. I pleaded with God to change me, to do anything He saw fit to save my marriage! Something inside me was dying with each failed attempt; like a flesh-eating cancer that slowly devours a body one painful nibble at a time.

Finally, I had to come to grips with the reality that I could not do anything to salvage the relationship without some co-operation. I found I could not continue to pretend all was well. I couldn't shield my children from the stress of the unhappy state of my marriage any longer. I stuck with it as long as I could and stayed true to my vows.

I also found out that nine years earlier, without my knowledge, CJ had called my dad and apologized for inviting everyone to the birthday party and said that we were wrong. I was furious! The only reason my dad came back to us was because CJ admitted we wronged him! Even though CJ was only trying to ease my sadness, I felt extremely betrayed and angry when he did it behind my back and didn't ever tell me about it.

I filed for divorce and that same evening, I called him down to the lower level of the house where the children were not in earshot. I explained that what I was about to tell him was not something that I wanted to do, but something I had to do because I couldn't live this anymore. I delivered my speech and stressed my reasons clearly.

He had brought me to this point by his actions and his attitudes over the last eighteen of the twenty-two years of our marriage. I told him that I loved him, but I could not and would not live without his reciprocated love and affection, conversation, companionship, and partnership, I felt like I was worthless to him. I would not continue to be his housekeeper, cook, and maid, and mother figure with no thanks or appreciation. I reminded him of how many times over the years that I had told him I was unhappy and he had ignored me. I reminded him of all the times I had begged him to go to counseling and finally when he did, he sat right in front of the counselor and laughed at me as I poured out all my hurt and pain. My needs were entirely ignored as I sacrificed every aspect of my entire life for my family. I would not let him continue to criticize, talk about our relationship problems, and put me down to our children behind my back, but refuse to take part in any discipline, making me appear as the "bad guy." I was tired of him using his early life as an excuse for the apathy, lack of co-operation, whining, pity parties, decisions, actions, and attitudes that contributed to the destruction of our marriage. I recalled that after ten years of marriage and an arranged suicide attempt in front of my pre-school daughter, he confessed all he did behind my back that were valid Biblical reasons for divorce. At that time, I chose to forgive him, put it all behind us, start over with his solemn promise of change. Here I was now at twenty-two years and found out that he had never changed and had continued his destructive behavior without any regards about the toll it would take on our marriage. And by the way, I wanted the house which I needed to raise our five children. He didn't say a word or react in any way.

I walked out of my marriage. It took twenty-two years of my life for me to learn that one person cannot save a relationship.

Each of us brought baggage into the marriage from our childhood. Each of us dealt with it differently. One can choose to use their past as an excuse for their behavior and attitudes or one can use the past as a tool and a learning experience to have a different and better outcome. CJ chose the first and I chose the second. I am far from perfect and I do take some responsibility for the failure of the marriage, but I truly believe in my heart that the marriage would have survived if CJ would have gotten on board to help save it. I never wanted it to fail.

No one will ever know or understand because they would have had to walk in my shoes all those years. I have peace in my heart knowing that the Lord knows the whole truth and knows how much I tried, the emotional pain I tolerated, and how many times I repeatedly forgave incidences that destroyed my trust and my self-esteem and ultimately shattered our marriage.

Where was God in all of this mess of mixed emotions and turmoil? Did I not go through enough in my childhood? Did I not deserve some peace and happiness? Why did He allow my marriage to fail? Why did He not do something to save my children and me from all this pain? Why did I spend over half my life trying to be everything I could be, only to be rejected? Why was I the "bad guy" when I was the one knocking myself out, arranging counseling sessions, and doing everything I could do to make it work?

I begged Him for answers. Crying my heart out in utter frustration and despair, I did feel His presence. I believe Jesus was right there sustaining me, giving me the strength to continue to care for my family. My Savior was the one who I knew loved me unconditionally, the one I could trust when I had lost all trust. I had to grasp His love to replace the feelings of rejection and low self-worth. I had to accept His peace when I could find none in myself. My questioning heart wrote the following words:

I Question Why

Cheryl Marie

The road is long; my path is dim.
I have no choice but to trust in Him.
My valley's deep; my river's dry
And deep within my heart I question why.

This emptiness is hard to bear.
Please let me feel your loving care.
It's hard to pray, instead I cry
And in my times of weakness, Lord, I question why.

Why Lord this trial I face?
Why Lord, where is your grace?
I need to feel your presence strong.
I need your hope, your love.
Please send it from above.
Help me to trust you, Lord, when I question why.

So all alone. I feel such pain.

I ask each day for strength again.

My spirit weeps, with tears I cry.

My dear and precious Lord, I question why.

"I am worn out from groaning; all night long I flood my bed with weeping and drench my couch with tears. My eyes grow weak with sorrow..." Psalm 6:6, 7 (NIV)

I cried until I had no tears left. I felt rejection so many times in my life. I didn't want to feel this hurt anymore. It is not a good feeling. I knew God loved me, but I still felt like I had no value or self-worth. My confidence was gone. I lost all trust. My spirit had been crushed and I was heartbroken and scared. How was I going to take care of the kids and make enough money to provide for them? My children were my motivation to keep on keeping on. I had to pull it together for them. "God help me! Please, help me," I prayed.

I felt sweet assurance as I heard Jesus speak these words to my heart.

I'll Carry You Through

Cheryl Marie

I heard you cry last night; I saw the tears you shed

As you laid your weary head upon your pillow.

I felt your sorrow and pain;
I saw the flame of hope die
As you questioned why, "why Lord, why me?"
Did you think I didn't see?
Did you think I didn't care?

And as the sun broke through,
I sensed your broken heart
As you grudgingly start the day in utter anguish.
I see your strength is gone,
So tired and filled with despair
As you wonder where you go from here.
Did you think I didn't see?
Did you think I didn't care?

My weary child, there is nothing I don't know.
My precious one, there's nothing I won't do for you.
Through the darkness I've been with you
And when life has dealt its bitter blows,
I've already been close beside you
To carry you through,
To carry you through, to carry you through.

I'm not tired, I'm not weary;
I have strength to carry,
To carry you through.

Through the darkness I've been with you
And when life has dealt its bitter blows,
I've already been close beside you
To carry you through,
To carry you through, to carry you through.

I had given up on men; I was going to make it on my own. I didn't need any man to support me. The Lord knows the whole truth of what happened and He would take care of me. At this point in my life, I realized that He was the only one who would never reject me because He loved me with a pure love that was unconditional. I didn't have to jump through hoops to earn His love.

I can still hear my dad saying, "There's not a good man on this earth; they're all the same; they're all good for nothing." He had his views and there was no reasoning with him. As I was growing up, he had given me such a hard time, not allowing me out of the house to socialize with my friends and dating was out of the question. I was never granted the joy of attending functions at school. I was never allowed to attend parties. I was never allowed to participate in sports. Friends were not allowed to come over on Friday nights. I was not even allowed to talk on the phone with the opposite sex. I was graduated from high school, had a full-time job, and he still controlled every area of my life. I never had the chance to date different guys to discover the qualities I wanted in a future husband. Even though I never believed what my dad drilled into my head, his words, his control, and overprotection was definitely a hindrance to my ability to choose the right mate for myself. One day on my school bus, I met a guy, fell in love and at the age of twenty, I married. I was alone and broken-hearted twenty-two years later.

My life seemed to be over, but I was determined to move on for the sake of my children. I didn't want this divorce, but because of the many underlying problems and CJ's lack of desire to resolve them, I reluctantly filed. I had gone for broke; I had given the marriage everything I had and had done every-thing I could possibly do to save it, but I still felt like a huge failure.

It was during this time that I experienced a severe blow that could have destroyed my faith. Surprisingly, it was from another Christian in leadership. Instead of compassion, understanding, and counsel, I was severely reprimanded for filing for divorce. This person had no idea what had happened in the marriage, but yet passed judgment.

"Let any one of you who is without sin be the first to throw a stone at her." John 8:7 (NIV)

The important point that I want to bring home is that none of us are without sin in our lives. Therefore, not one of us can sit in judgment of someone else. We haven't walked where they have walked or been through what they have been through. We do not know "the rest of the story." Jesus calls us to show compassion, love, and forgiveness.

I had to forgive as God calls us to forgive.

And when you stand praying, if you hold anything against anyone, forgive them, so that your Father in heaven may forgive you your sins." Mark 11:25 (NIV)

Even though I said that I forgave this person, it took time to feel full forgiveness within my heart.

Chapter 11

Prince Charming to My Rescue

Lonely, devastated, needy, and vulnerable, I started my new life with my five hurting children. I was scared, but I don't know why because I had done everything myself for twenty-two years. I worked hard every day and took care of the kids and when they were all safely tucked into bed, I cried myself to sleep. This was my life. Every day was the same. I shed a lot of tears, but never in front of the children. So, they thought I wasn't affected by the divorce. In the meantime, their father was just laying it on thick of how he was hurting so bad and how could I do this to our family and he did nothing to deserve this. The children knew no different because I never fought with their dad about anything. I stuffed it all. All I had to say to him was said in private and it went through one ear and out the other with no expression or empathy at all. The last thing I wanted to do was put the kids in the middle. No, I wouldn't make them go through the turmoil that I experienced growing up. I did not try to defend myself to my angry children. I did not talk negative against their father. I remained silent, stuffed my pain, and prayed

God would take care of the situation. I believed it was the right thing to do, but it devastated me.

Help Me Lift My Hands and Praise

Cheryl Marie

When the way seems dark and the road seems long
And in my heart, there is no song,
Help me, Lord, to lift my hands and praise.
When there is no hope and all is lost,
Seems like serving you isn't worth the cost
Help me Lord, to lift my hands and praise.

Let me lift my hands and praise;
My heart to the Heavens raise
Glory to Jesus, the one who gave
His life for my pain-His blessings fall like rain
Help me, Lord, to lift my hands and praise
You deserve to receive all the praise I have to give
For there is power in my worship
For the life I have to live

Change my heart, change my mind,
The joy, deep down, cause me to find.

Help me, Lord, to lift my hands and praise.

Light my path, help me rise,

Help me focus on the prize.

Help me, Lord, to lift my hands and praise.

Months passed and Prince Charming came into the picture. Dan was a tall, large framed, boisterous guy with a very dominant personality. In the beginning, he intruded my little arena like a bull stampeding the red flag. I didn't like him at first and I made a conscious effort to try to slow down the fast-moving runaway train on which he had taken me as a reluctant passenger.

From our first date. he relentlessly pursued me. This was all new to me. For at least eighteen years, I rarely felt like CJ even cared if I was there or not. Dan was attentive to my chil-dren and took an interest in their lives and activities. He cooked dinner for us, helped me cook, or took us out to eat almost every day. There were very few days in my whole marriage to CJ that I didn't have to plan and/or prepare dinner and he never cooked with me. We rarely ate out because we just couldn't afford it. Dan wouldn't let me carry anything heavy or do anything difficult. I never had help with carrying children, groceries, or anything. I took care of just about everything even the most difficult chores. I couldn't help but compare him to CJ. Dan bought me gifts and sent me flowers. CJ, very few gifts and no flowers. Dan hung on my every word and CJ wouldn't even make eye contact during our infrequent conver-sations. Dan took care of my house and my vehicle. CJ, rarely. Dan stated over and over that he loved me and I was the one he had been searching for. CJ hadn't touched me sexually or non-sexually since the birth of the twins or said "I love you" for a decade or more. Dan

The Sun Will Shine Again

believed and tried to convince me that God had sent him to take care of me, but I didn't have a clue what that meant. Even from my childhood, I had always been the one taking care of everyone else. I was the caretaker in my marriage. This was so foreign to me.

In all the months that we dated, we never had a disagreement. Dan just stepped in and took charge. I finally found a man who was capable of making decisions. I thought that was great. I went along with just about everything he thought we should or shouldn't do. I was relieved of all the pressure of decisions and at the time, it felt pretty freeing.

Dan persistently pursued me and after a while, the showering of phone calls, flowers, dinners, the interest in me and involvement in my family began to feel good. Life was so much easier. I had someone to share my responsibilities. I never experienced that before either. I was always the one doing everything for everybody else.

I talked with Dan many times about my commitment and relationship with Jesus Christ and how important that was to me. Even though he was of another denomination, he attended church regularly and claimed he had accepted the Lord and believed as I did. Being assured that we were both Christians, I started to consider that maybe God had sent him.

Over a period of time, I listened to him talk about work and friends. I heard stories about events of the past. I pondered as he told me that his lying first wife had filed a "Protection from Abuse" order against him during the marriage and he had done nothing to

103

constitute that order. How wrongly he had been accused! She was the reason that he was so deep in debt and his credit was ruined. I took an interest in the way he handled life's situations. I considered his thoughts, views, and opinions. I listened how he bragged about the domination he had over his working partner and what he did to instill fear to make sure he got his own way. He explained that when he was young and immature, how a car was following him too closely and how it had angered him. At the next stop sign, Dan bragged how he had thrown his car in park, jumped out and kicked in the headlight before he sped off into the night. He spoke of the night he drove into the parking lot and destroyed the lighted business sign of a doctor that he thought had an interest in his wife. He would never even think about doing anything like that now! Also, in those days of youthful foolishness, he talked with an arrogant pride about how he would abuse cats because of his hatred of them. I heard all the off-color jokes he thought were funny, and noted the kind of questionable TV shows he watched. The Holy Spirit began to deal with me and God warned me about going any further with the relationship. I knew I needed to end it. It did not feel right anymore. I knew he was not sent from God to take care of me and I had a choice to make.

I was still hurting terribly from my failed marriage. I was needy and love-starved. I was weak and worn and I surely wasn't thinking clearly. I reasoned that he was so open telling me all those things; Surely, he wasn't the same person that he was in his younger days. Everyone has done things that they were ashamed of; Dan trusted me enough to share even the bad things!

I considered all the good things Dan had done for us. Life was so much easier. He had a good job with great benefits and my children would be taken care of. The responsibilities I had carried in my childhood and in my former marriage would be shared and I would be free from the heavy load that was wearing me down physically and mentally. He spent most of his free time with me and desired a relationship. It felt so good to finally be wanted and to be needed. A happy family was in my grasp and that was what I wanted more than anything.

Unfortunately, I made the choice to do what "I" thought I should do. Being in a very vulnerable state in my life from the pain and rejection of my marriage to CJ, I looked to a man to take care of me when I should have been looking and trusting in my Heavenly Father. God will step aside and allow you to do your own thing. He is a gentleman and He does not force His will on you. I made one of the biggest mistakes of my life when I mistook control for love. I take complete and total responsibility for my disastrous decision. I am so sorry that I did not listen to the Holy Spirit's warning. It must have hurt my Heavenly Father to watch His child suffer the consequences of her bad choices.

Chapter 12

A Different Kind of Happy

Ever After

The day before our wedding, Dan stopped by my house in a brand spanking new, metallic dark blue truck with all the bells and whistles. He had never hinted about or discussed the purchase with me. There was not even room for all of my children. Never having to ask for anyone's permission to buy a vehicle before, he was thoroughly confused and couldn't understand why in the world I was so upset. I tried to explain that neither of us should purchase anything of that value without talking about it with each other. He just didn't see what the big deal was, but reluctantly took it back the next morning. Stunned and hurt at what he did, I couldn't understand why he was the one sulking. That was our first disagreement ever and I caused it because I made a big deal over him buying a vehicle without talking to me. He was angry about the whole episode, but we proceeded with the marriage anyway. *What in the world was I thinking?* I believe now that the Lord was trying to show me, before it was too late, that I was making a grave mistake. *What in the world was I thinking?*

Early on our wedding day, Dan took the one and one-half hour trip and returned the truck. The dealer took it back minus one thousand dollars. Then Dan financed several thousand more than he had already financed and chose a fully loaded full size extra-long dark red luxury van which resulted in a payment higher than my mortgage. When he returned, he went out of his way to assure me that he landed an excellent deal and he hoped I was satisfied. I had no words.

That afternoon, we had a small ceremony with family and friends. I accepted what was done because I couldn't do anything about it anyway. Dan seemed ok with it all, too. All in all, it was a nice wedding and we left early that evening for Pittsburgh to catch a plane the next morning.

Evidently still upset about my confrontation, Dan pouted on our honeymoon. He had made plans to take me to Las Vegas. I had never been there before and really didn't know what to expect. I was shocked at the atmosphere of some of the hotels and casinos. I felt like I was in hell itself in a few of the attractions of the city. He tried to force me to go to places and take part in things that did not feel comfortable in my spirit. I was shocked that he felt at ease, considering the fact he proclaimed he was walking with Christ also. When I got up and left a very offensive venue that was labeled as "family" entertainment and refused to go back inside, He called me filthy names. He told me I was not living in the real world and that I existed like an ostrich with my head in the sand. Dan then threatened to leave me in Nevada without any money or my luggage. I spent a lot of time in the hotel room alone. I seriously thought about ending the marriage when we got home from our honeymoon. My second mistake was listening to and accepting his apologies and promises that it wouldn't happen again and that our marriage would get better.

Better? I don't think so! The situation did not change. My children were belittled and called names, told they were stupid, treated cruelly and unfairly, and made to feel worthless. There were times of physical abuse also. I consistently spoke up to protect my family from these attacks and that's when the wrath was turned on me. Fear filled our days. I developed chronic stomach conditions because of the tension. My children were greatly affected and experienced physical symptoms caused by extreme stress. When I heard his vehicle pulling into the driveway, I became instantly ill for I never knew who the "victim" would be that evening or what would set him off. Migraine headaches became an everyday occurrence. My hands shook uncontrollably from the anxiety. We were isolated from my side of the family, but forced to visit his. On these occasions, he demeaned my children and me in front of his parents, brothers and sisters. Then he laughed at the mocking statements he had made. I wasn't allowed to associate with my friends. He controlled every penny of our money from all the accounts, spending foolishly on whatever he wanted. When I said anything that differed from his thoughts on any matter, he would not give me money for food or bills. Since his credit was destroyed before we married, he took all my credit cards and all spending was in his control. I had obtained the highest level of credit on each card since I had always paid all my debtors in full each month on time. Now each card was maxed due to his spending habits.

During our seven and one-half year marriage, Dan had left us five times. He returned each time crying, with gifts and apologies, and promised to change. Weeks before he left each time, he locked me out of my own garage and removed what he wanted from my home and stored the items in a locked utility trailer inside the locked garage. Tables, chairs, clothing, important paperwork, even pictures from our wall disappeared when I went to bed or when I was in another room of my large home. I lived each day, seeing what he was doing but pretending I didn't. As he packed his stash, it was difficult to hide my anger, and it was stressful not knowing when he would leave. I felt my children and I would be in greater danger if I said anything about it. Eventually, the day came and he went on some kind of self-created rampage, stormed out of the house and hooked up his trailer and left. The day had been previously planned because his parents, who lived almost four hours away would be parked in their car outside waiting to help him. He had already rented an apartment with a security deposit and bought what he needed, using my credit cards, to set up housekeeping. The next day to three weeks later, he would come back home, empty-handed, having given away everything he had purchased or had taken with him. Then he went and bought, again with my credit cards, new replacements for all the items he had given away. If you multiply the cost of his tantrums times five, you would have some understanding of the debt that was accumulated. I took him back and forgave him five times. Isn't that what good Christians are supposed to do?

"Then Peter came to Jesus and asked, "Lord, how many times shall I forgive my brother or sister who sins against me? Up to seven times? Jesus answered, "I tell you, not seven times, but seventy-seven times" Matthew 18:21,22 (NIV)

Each time, after stalking, flowers, letters, crying phone calls, and apologies, I forgave him and allowed him to return home. Dan agreed to the conditions I set forth. He promised he would treat me with respect, be nice to my children, stop his foolish spending, and

I would be given an equal voice in our relationship. He put forth the effort to be on his best behavior for a while, but soon enough, the abuse started all over again.

We had been married about two years when I needed a cervical disk fusion in my neck. I had been in a car accident five years before. The time had come when all other means of treatment had failed. His parents arrived the night before to watch the children. Dan picked a fight that afternoon. He was in a horrible mood that evening and he continued arguing the next morning on the two-hour drive to the hospital. I had endured his screaming, his out of control anger, his threats, and his abusive remarks for the entire trip. When we finally arrived, my mental and physical condition was not conducive to surgery. My blood pressure was elevated from all the trauma and I shook uncontrollably. Having stress induced asthma, I struggled to breathe. I had a severe migraine, I was dizzy, and my stomach was sick. Being in a safe environment caused me to stabilize after a few hours and the surgery was done.

My stay in the hospital was a few days and the time came to return home. I was instructed to recover on a recliner for three weeks wearing a neck brace whenever I slept or got out of the chair. With or without the neck brace, any sudden or impulsive movement could cause permanent harm, even paralysis. I was warned to move with extreme care until the cadaver bone inserted between the disks fused and healed completely. Disconnected from the morphine drip that had kept my pain to a minimum, I was dressed and wheeled to the car for our trip home. The effects of the narcotic medication still had me groggy and unable to think clearly or to be physically independent. All I can clearly remember about that two-hour ride back home is Dan's intense screaming and the deliberate back and forth jerking of our automobile. In a daze, I recall thinking that he was intentionally trying to damage what was corrected in surgery. I prayed and asked God to help me and to protect me. I was trapped, scared, and helpless in my small compact car. At one point, under the influence of the drugs and the severe abuse in such a contained area, I tried to open the car door. I didn't care what happened to me; I had to get away. He grabbed me with such force and jerked the car so bad that I knew I was totally at his mercy.

"Answer me when I call to you, my righteous God. Give me relief from my distress; have mercy on me and hear my prayer." Psalm 4:1 (NIV)

When I returned home, I followed doctor's orders and made my bed in the living room recliner. I was happy to be there instead of having to share a bed with him after what he had just put me through.

One evening a few weeks later, while I was in the chair relaxing without my neck brace on, he became enraged once more. I sat in fear as I watched him pacing the floor and screaming. Because of the narcotic pain medicine that I was still taking, I couldn't respond quickly and surely did not want to say anything to make the situation worse! My silence angered him more and the next thing I remember is the leg rest of my recliner being lifted and tipped up so high that the chair fell backward onto the floor and my head slammed against the wall. My painful screams stopped him in his tracks and I saw the terror in his eyes.

I insisted I go to the hospital emergency room, but he would only take me if I agreed to keep quiet about "the accident" that had happened. As the nurse questioned me, he looked straight at me. I could feel his warning threat even though I made no eye contact with him. I told her that I fell. She looked at Dan, looked at me and said, "Now tell me what really happened." Knowing that someone was on to him, I was tempted to blurt out the whole truth and nothing but the truth. That is, until I felt his hand around mine with his tightening grip. I then said, "I fell." She left the room sighing and shaking her head. She knew. I know she knew.

During one of the five separations, I went to work for a large department store. I had only been there two months. At some point each day, Dan would come in and stalk me as I was doing my job. He would find the department where I was working and would stand and watch me. Sometimes he tried to talk to me. He would be in the parking lot when I had a lunch break. He would be waiting when my shift was over, begging for forgiveness and asking to come home.

While walking through the storeroom of the business early one morning, I was involved in a freak accident. A young man moving a tall ladder knocked down a thirty-five-pound mountain bike from the twenty-five-foot ceiling. The bike struck me with such force that I literally saw stars. The intense, unexpected, and heavy blow separated my shoulder, tore my rotator cuff, and damaged nerves in my neck. After landing on my shoulder, it bounced off my leg, shredding my Achilles tendon.

Since he was my husband, Dan was called when I was taken to the hospital for treatment. He acted exceptionally con-cerned and adamantly insisted that he was coming back home to take care of me and the kids. I was in no condition to argue with him.

I spent the next thirty months in bed as an invalid. I couldn't walk unassisted and I couldn't move freely because of the relentless severe pain in every part of my body. I endured painful shoulder surgery and couldn't recover. I developed fibromyalgia as a result of the trauma of the accident and the stress at home. As I lay in bed, highly medicated, I could hear the constant mistreatment of my children and was powerless to protect them. I was so helpless, hopeless, and depressed. Overwhelming sadness engulfed me as I felt so alone and I blamed myself. Nagging guilt and condemnation began to weigh me down even more. I deserved everything that had happened.

"Be merciful to me, Lord, for I am in distress; my eyes grow weak with sorrow, my soul and body with grief. My life is consumed by anguish and my years by groaning; my strength fails because of my affliction, and my bones grow weak." Psalm 31:9, 10 (NIV)

Only I, with the power of Christ within me, could change my depressing attitude and my disheartening situation. With everything in me, I rebuked the persistent accusations and continual taunts from the enemy. I begged God for forgiveness for ruining, not only my life, but the lives of my children. I asked him for another chance to live in His will, not mine.

"Have mercy on me, O God, according to your unfailing love; according to your great compassion blot out my transgressions. Wash away all my iniquity and cleanse me from sin." Psalm 51:1,2 (NIV)

"Create in me a pure heart, O God, and renew a steadfast spirit within me. Do not cast me from your presence or take your Holy Spirit from me. Restore to me the joy of your salvation and grant me a willing spirit to sustain me." Psalm 51:10-12 (NIV)

What a wonderful and forgiving God I serve; a God of second chances! I began to feel His sweet presence, His glorious power, and His magnificent strength. One day, I decided that I would quit taking medication and would rely on my God to raise me up; I was determined to get better. That day of reckoning was the first step of the healing process for my body, even though Dan's abuse continued. I began therapy to learn to balance and walk again, normally and unassisted. I read the Word of God, applied it to my life, stood on the precious promises, and put my trust in my Lord.

"But you, LORD, are a shield around me, my glory, the One who lifts my head high. I call out to the LORD, and he answers me from his holy mountain." Psalm 3:3,4 (NIV)

"The LORD is a refuge for the oppressed, a strong-hold in times of trouble. Those who know your name trust in you, for you, LORD, have never forsaken those who seek you." Psalm 9:9,10 (NIV)

"In my distress I called to the Lord; I cried to my God for help. From his temple he heard my voice; my cry came before him, into his ears." Psalm 18: 6 (NIV)

"God is our refuge and strength, and ever-present help in trouble. Therefore, we will not fear...." Psalm 46: 1,2 (NIV)

Over time, I regained my strength and returned to living my life as best as I could under the trying and wearisome circumstances. I had to be "on guard" continually and be careful not to voice the slightest hint of opposition about anything Dan decided to do. His raging temper was dangerously impulsive and I never knew, without warning, when he could snap.

I couldn't state my opinion on any decision he made. He had bought and traded in so many new vehicles in seven and one-half years that the payments were double my house payment. Most of the time we were married, we had three vehicles in our driveway. I wasn't permitted to drive the cars, only his old 1977 work truck. Dan gave away expensive tools after he used them for whatever project he was doing and then went out and bought the same tool so he would own it new. He spent thousands of dollars foolishly and I couldn't reason with him. I had two credit cards that he maxed out. People have asked me why I gave him the credit cards and why I didn't stop him from using them. They cannot understand unless they have been where I was. If I would have destroyed the cards, I feared the unknown, but severe consequences. I could not stop him from using them for the same reason. He drained all the bank accounts to control me.

I felt like I was living inside a large black cloud. There are no words in the English language to begin to describe the depth of pain, insecurity, confusion, fear, helplessness, stress, and anger that I felt. I was isolated from my friends and family for so long that I felt like I had no one. Not a word could I share for fear that he would find out and hurt me or my sweet, innocent children. My mind was a blur and I lacked the rationale to devise a plan to save myself or my children. I would struggle and do what I had to do to safely survive, leaning on the Lord.

"Come to me, all you who are weary and burdened, and I will give you rest." Matthew 11:28 (NIV)

This scripture spoke to my heart. As I meditated on the faithfulness of the Lord, I penned the following words:

Come unto Me

Cheryl Marie

Do you know that the affliction
That you're going through right now
Is allowed by God and is working for your good?
Don't think for a moment that he's left you all alone
And He could reach right down
And change it if He would.

But you haven't learned the lesson
That He wants you to learn
And the reaction to your problem
Is not what it should be.
His mercy and His grace are at your beckon call;

That's why, in His Word, Jesus says come unto me.

Come unto me, my child, I love you so.
Come unto me, my child, please always know.
I will never forsake you, you're always in my care
And I will not allow you more than you can bear.

So have peace in your storm,
Keep my words in your heart.
Each promise I have written, it is true.
Know I'll never leave you in good times and in bad
And you have my Holy Spirit to comfort you.

I had extreme guilt, sorrow, and remorse for the decision I had made to marry Dan. I could feel my spirit grieving and my emotions sliding on a downhill spiral, like an out of control car going down a steep slope on ice. I could feel the toll that all the stress was taking on my mind and body. Nothing I could say or do was right. The intense screaming, the disgusting obscenities, the vulgar name-calling, the demeaning slurs, the relentless mocking, and the whole pessimistic tone of our disastrous relationship was sucking the very life right out of me.

As a child I used to jump rope saying:

"Sticks and stones may break my bones, but names will never hurt me."

What a lie that is! I knew from my childhood life and incidences that words do hurt and they do cause extreme dam-age. No one has the right to inflict pain on another person by verbal or physical assault regardless of the circumstances. Through my painful experience, I have found that the scars from carelessly spoken words are harder to heal than the scars inflicted physically. It is as if the abusive destructive vocabulary becomes engraved on walls of your brain and the enemy constantly and consistently uses those lies to defeat and taunt you. Until you accept God's truth and the value He has on your life, you will have no victory over the haunting echoes in your mind.

"The tongue has the power of life and death." Psalm 18:21 (NIV)

I eventually stopped saying anything at all. I had with-drawn to a deep self-preservation mode. For my children's and my own protection, I shut down all unnecessary communication and I prayerfully surrendered the marriage to the Lord. I was done trying; maybe this would bring some semblance of peace to our home and relationship. Even though there is no comparison with my suffering and the suffering of our Lord, I thought about how Jesus responded when He was mistreated.

"When they hurled their insults at him, he did not retaliate; when he suffered, he made no threats. Instead he entrusted himself to him who judges justly." I Peter 2:23 (NIV)

I read my Bible without fail even though the stress overload was hindering my understanding. I knew that God was still there and

I continued to reach out to Him. Even though the words hurt tremendously, I endured Dan's mocking of my Christian faith with silence. His disrespectful slurs and crude demeaning comments about my Lord cut through my heart like a sharp knife and tears would sting my eyes as I closed them tightly to avoid their escape to my cheeks.

Dan bought a brand-new compact car for me to use. I was happy that I didn't have to drive the big work truck any more, but unhappy about still another decision he made on his own against my wishes. One evening, Scott needed to borrow my car to visit his fiancé who lived about a ten minute drive from my house. Scott had moved out a few months before because of the way Dan treated him. He had his own apartment, but couldn't yet afford a car. Dan wasn't home and I gave Scott permission to use my car for a couple of hours. After he left, Dan returned home and burst forcefully through the door. He demanded me to tell him where my car was. My heart pounded and my stomach felt sick as I tried to control the trembling of every part of my body. Sitting at my computer and without taking my eyes from the screen, I told him calmly that my son borrowed it for a short while. Dan went into a wild rage, screaming, swearing, and punching the walls. He stormed out of the house on that dark night, slammed the door, kicked the fence surrounding the deck, and screamed obscenities and threats as he stomped to his car. I heard the screeching of the tires and I feared what he would do. Almost instantaneously, Jillian and her fiancé came into the house concerned for our safety. They had been talking in the car across the street and had witnessed his explosion of uncontrollable rage. For the time being, we were safe, but I had to warn Scott. I just knew that was where he was going. Dan showed up at the apartment of his fiancé, ranting, raving, banging on the door and demanding the keys to my car. Scott would not open the door and threatened to call the police if he didn't leave. As my son watched from the window, Dan threw open the hood of my car, pulled every wire loose, disconnected the plugs and hoses, slammed the hood shut, and peeled out of the parking lot. Scott called and told me what he had done and I was just thankful that he didn't harm my son. Now I was shaking uncontrollably because I knew he would be coming home. I prayed and asked my Lord for His protection.

"If you say, The LORD is my refuge, and you make the Most High your dwelling, no harm will overtake you, no disaster will come near your tent." Psalm 91: 9-10 (NIV)

Dan came in quietly, got a shower, and acted as if noth-ing ever happened. I was so nervous and scared that night just waiting for his explosive anger. His silence had become just as threatening as the volatile, hot headed fits of rage. The next day, Dan came home unexpectedly during his working hours and asked nicely if I would drive him out to get my car. He admitted what he did and he needed some time to fix it and then I would have to drive it back home as he returned to work. I mustered the courage and told him that I refused to go and added, boldly, that I didn't care if I had a car to drive or not. I refused to condone his behavior by helping him undo the damage he had done. There I said it! I waited for the wrath, but instead he left quietly. The car was home by that evening and I have no idea how it got there

.

I lived for months with little response to the outrageous screaming episodes except for the times I had to come to the defense my children. My mental condition was getting worse. Despair and anguish filled my days and nights. I didn't know what to do with all the frustration and intense pain. I honestly desired and attempted to please the Lord in each situation, but nothing changed. I tried to rest in the Lord as best I could. I realized He was my only hope of ever getting through the awful mess I had created for my family.

"I can do all this through him who gives me strength." Phil 4:13 (NIV)

"Yes, my soul, find rest in God; my hope comes from him. Truly he is my rock and my salvation; he is my fortress. I will not be shaken." Psalm 62:5,6 (NIV)

"Never will I leave you-never will I forsake you. The Lord is my helper; I will not be afraid. What can mere mortals do to me?" Hebrews 13:5,6 (NIV)

A journal entry I wrote during this time speaks of my despondency and desolation.

How many times will I have to feel this awful frustration, this gnawing in my stomach, this absolute helpless state? I cannot express my pain or more pain is piled on! I cannot protect my children or they are hurt worse! I am not even respected enough to be listened to about anything! Why? Why is it this way? I cannot speak, I can only continue to watch pained little faces that tear out my very soul. I take a deep breath and suck it in and ask God to heal their little broken hearts. My misery and anger builds. I draw inward, yet forced to go on pretending it doesn't hurt, pretending I believe all the praise administered to himself, when deep down inside, my very being cries for respect and companionship. My heart yearns for someone who can accept how I feel without putting the kids and me through hell itself just because I speak of the pain we're feeling. After all the damage is done and tempers let out all the dirt that tears apart relationships beyond repair, then and only then, can I express myself. It brings no consolation because I am so upset, it doesn't come out lovingly and I am not given any resemblance of understanding. His apology resolves it somewhat until it happens again and then it starts over with the same cycle. GOD HAVE MERCY; STOP THIS CYCLE! All I want is to be listened to, always, not after all respect and trust is destroyed again. Why can't I be respected enough to say anything of the pain I feel at his words to me and my kids? Hasn't enough damage been done to us all? GOD HELP ME! Why is any intimate feeling I've ever shared thrown up to me? How can I ever trust after promises are broken time and time again? How can I be a loving wife when I am treated with no respect for what I feel and stabbed with the very things I share? God, I feel like I can't go on like this anymore. I am sick all the time, I'm unhappy, I'm depressed, and my life is constant stress! How can he be so blind to what his pride and hard heart is doing to us? How can he say he loves us and make us feel so worthless? God, change anything in me that is not right and give me the strength to stand up to his inflictions. Help me to forgive. Thank you, Jesus.

The situation was growing gravely worse. I walked around the house in a daze, a state of total numbness. I eventually lost my will to live. At the end, I began to unflinchingly approach Dan in his raging tantrum and say, "Go ahead and kill me. You would be doing me a favor." I would say this daringly, defiantly, and fearlessly as I stared at him straight in his piercing, threatening eyes.

Declaring that I just didn't care anymore if he hurt me, provoked him to act more violently. He loved it when I was afraid of him. My fear gave him great satisfaction and a sense of power.

Losing my fear and becoming defiant escalated the violence. Trying to regain control and establish his place of supreme authority, he would repeatedly and forcefully push against me with his large two hundred sixty-five-pound frame until I was hurled into a wall or I would fall backwards over a small table. A six-foot two-inch man with a fifty-two-inch chest was no comparison to my five foot one and one half-inch small frame. After I would pick myself up off the floor and glare rebelliously at him, he would put up both hands and say with a sneering voice, "I never laid a hand on you!" The same remark was repeated when he hurled a small table at me and it broke into pieces. He always destroyed belongings that were the most sentimental to me. When his tantrum escalated, I ran to a room to escape the next unexpected push, shove, or hurling object. Our bedroom was the only room upstairs that he had installed a lock on the door. One day, I ran to that room and locked the door to escape his rage. He ran after me and busted the lock right off the door which, in turn ripped out a chunk of the woodwork from the door frame. He continued to scream and harass me, nose to nose, as he held me down on the bed. If he pinned me against the wall, he would pull back his fist and swing with all his might. I felt the rush of air as I closed my eyes. Sometimes his swinging fists made holes in the walls. Dan fixed them when he returned home to make things right after the separations, but another hole was made before much time passed. Many times, he trapped me into a corner and screamed in my face until I lowered myself into a fetal position on the floor and covered my head and ears. He forced himself on me when he was in a rage. He did, however, stop this when I threatened a rape charge. There were also other incidences where I would run outside even in my pajamas. A couple times I grabbed the keys to the car and left for a while. I thought that my absence ended the tantrum.

I later learned that during these episodes, my children were terrorized and had to hide. Dan would find them, and con-tinued to yell and take his anger out on them. This brings such pain and sorrow to my heart. I would have never left if I had had any idea he would do that to my children. I didn't know anything about that for years. Nothing I could say could ever express how sorry I am to my precious loved ones that suffered during this marriage.

Abuse is something that you have to experience to actually understand. Your mind is on overload and decisions are made spontaneously to survive.

I was so broken. I wasn't angry with God, just myself. I knew I had disregarded what God had told me. We suffered dreadfully for seven and one-half years. All I could do now is pray.

"Lord I bring my family to you. I ask your forgiveness for what I have done. I have learned my lesson. My children and I need your healing. We need your restoration. I make you this promise today. You will be first in my life from this day forth. You will be my husband, my provider, my friend. The desire of my heart is to help other people who have experienced disappointment and pain. Use all that I have experienced for your glory, Lord."

"Therefore, since we have been justified through faith, we have peace with God through our Lord Jesus Christ, through whom we have gained access by faith into the grace in which we now stand. And we boast in the hope of the glory of God. Not only so, but we also glory in our sufferings because we know that suffering produces perseverance, perseverance, character, and character, hope. And hope does not put us to shame, because

God's love has been poured out into our hearts through the Holy Spirit, who has been given to us." Romans 5:1-5 (NIV)

I stood on this promise. I believed with all my heart. He, the Lord Jesus Christ, is my only hope to ever escape.

Dan came to me and apologized tearfully begging me to "start over" with him. "Let's put everything behind us," he said. "I'm sorry. I didn't mean to hurt you. I have learned how sensitive you are and now I know the way I talk to you offends you. Please give us one more chance. I will change. I promise. We are going to refinance the house and get all the debt consolidated to a lower payment. I want to pay off all your credit cards." Dan had apologized and tried to change numerous times before, but had never offered to change his spending habits or to pay off our debt. I wasn't thinking very clearly, but I agreed to go because he seemed sincere about how badly he felt.

He had inquired about consolidation and called me one afternoon to see if I was free to go with him. I agreed. I knew nothing about refinancing and consolidation and I couldn't question him anyway about anything he did. We arrived at an office in a town nearby and Dan told me to wait in the car and he would go and do all the paperwork. About twenty minutes had passed and he knocked on my car window and motioned for me to come with him because they needed a signature. On the way up the elevator, he was elated and told me that the payments would be considerably lower and we would be free of the heavy burden of debt. I entered the office and was greeted warmly by a man in a suit behind a desk who wasted no time in asking me to sign on the line where he had placed a big "X." I did and Dan shook hands and thanked the man. As he closed the door behind me, he sniggered and said, "Ha, now my name is on your house."

He had no intention of reducing our debt. His motive was to get his name on my home.

Chapter 13

The Final Episode

"The righteous cry out, and the Lord hears them; he delivers them from all their troubles. The Lord is close to the brokenhearted and saves those who are crushed in spirit. A righteous person may have many troubles, but the Lord delivers him from them all; he protects all his bones, not one of them will be broken." Psalm 34:17-20 (NIV)

Even when we get ourselves in terrible situations because we ignore His voice, God is still in control. I thank him for His protection on that last day of my awful marriage.

"Do not be far from me, for trouble is near and there is no one to help." Psalm 22:11 (NIV)

With great anxiety, I was on guard for I anticipated what was coming. Dan had been storing up his stash in the gar-age. His clothing had been in boxes in the closet for months. After promising so many times that he would change, after promising that he was there to stay, I had become wiser and had not believed his lies anymore. I had learned the cycle well. Our life together would never get better. I had not lost faith that God could turn this marriage around, but I knew that Dan's heart was hard. He had no intention of ever admitting that he was controlling and had anger issues. He had too much pride.

During our time together, he would not go to counseling with me. I started to go a few months before that final day and he was in approval of that. He was glad I was going! Dan believed that the counselor would set me straight, put me in my rightful place, and then, we could go on with our marriage. She would tell me that I should be thankful to have a good guy that took care of me. She would tell me that Dan, as my husband, is the ruler of the household, that he brought in the money, and he could spend it as he pleased. She would also explain to me that I caused him to explode. It was all my fault that he acted like he did. I attended counseling sessions for a month or so, until the counselor saw the whole picture and understood what my children and I were going through.

In one of my sessions, she told me to ask Dan if he would come and share his side and he thought that was a good idea because who knows what I had said to make him look bad! After all, I was the reason that he lost his temper. I was responsible for all his behavior. One evening, Dan and I drove over together and we were waiting in the office for our appointment time. After collecting information about the happenings of the week, she called him in to join us. I sat quietly with my eyes on the floor as she allowed him to share his side.

When he paused, the counselor began to question him about some of the information that I had given her. Dan arrogantly admitted to most of what I had said he did, but he did not agree with me that his rules were unreasonable and his expectations were unrealistic. He proudly told her that if my children left a light on when they walked out of a room, even for a few minutes, he confiscated the bulb and wouldn't give it back. He boasted how he kept the house in order by constantly "encouraging" my kids to put away their shoes and book bags the second they walked in the door or they would have them taken away until he saw fit to return them. The whole truth was that if my kids left their shoes or book bags in view, their belongings were thrown down the steps and as they ran to retrieve the shoes, coat, or bag, they were threatened, belittled, and called vulgar names. The shoes had to be neatly lined up in their closets or they saw his wrath. He pompously disclosed that he often would call the children together and say that he had lots of change in his pocket and they could have it. He would count out each child's share and would purposely give different amounts to each. Sometimes one child would get nothing. If the child questioned why they received less or nothing, he would take their share away. If the child accepted it without protest and gave up his right to speak up for himself or herself, they were not reprimanded. Dan confidently stated that this was teaching them lessons of trust, knowledge of who was in control, and appreciation for what they had. As a stepfather, it was his duty to continuously stalk my son in hopes of catching him doing anything that was against the rules. Dan's degrading and condemning accusations were just his style of discipline. He had a right to "keep my children in line" in any cold, unloving and demeaning way he saw fit, without me taking their side. And the black and blue marks all over Brock's body had appeared from friendly rough housing and he was just trying to bond with the boy. Dan even proudly stated that he complimented my son on how much pain he could endure as he walked away with the bruises of the "fun." When he forced Sheila to run with a painful dislocated hip while calling her a wimp, he said he was "toughening her up." His drill sergeant commands and humiliating remarks to my children were teaching them lessons they needed to learn. The counselor asked him about the time that he entered the family room carrying a tray of plastic dishes and utensils. Brock was getting a motherly back rub from his big sister, Jillian, and they were in a conversation. Dan gruffly demanded that Brock take the tray downstairs "NOW." Brock proceeded to finish the thought about which he and his sister were conversing. Approximately ten to fifteen seconds elapsed before Dan threw the tray at Brock. He viciously screamed at him, as my son scrambled to pick up the scattered dishes. Brock's character was attacked. He was a lazy, disgusting, a good for nothing moron (just like his dad) and he was going to learn that when Dan said "MOVE," you "MOVE." He also big-headedly admitted to telling my children they were stupid and dumb. He bragged about how he had gone to "talk" to Brock in his room. He had asked me for permission to do so and I had made him agree that he would be civil and talk respectfully. A few minutes later, I heard thrashing and screaming. I ran up to my son's room and saw the results of his civil talk. As I entered, I witnessed Dan pinning Brock against the wall with his shirt ripped and blood pouring out of his mouth and nose. He had barged through the door, threw my son across the bed, kicked him, and then picked him up and slammed him into the wall. He told Brock that I knew what he was going to do and had given him permission to go up and "straighten him up." Brock glared at me as I pleaded with him to believe me that I would never do that! My son left and moved in with his dad shortly after. I was crushed! But at least he would not be abused anymore by the tyrant I lived with. Dan admitted that he didn't have feelings for my children, but they were part of the package when he married me. He also admitted to the incident with Scott when he disconnected all the wires in my car. He explained that even though he purchased the car for me to drive, it was technically his car since he paid for it and I had no right to lend it to my son. Dan was secure and confident and talked in a calm and normal tone, as he elaborated on his amazing parenting skills.

The conversation then came to his treatment of me. He justified purchasing anything he pleased because he made the money. I had no right to have an opinion of or deny him any-thing he desired. He supported me and my children and I was just plain ungrateful! Dan warranted taking every cent from the house and emptying all the bank accounts and leaving the bills unpaid to teach me that I had no right to voice my opinion about his spending. He quickly added that when I learned my lesson and kept my mouth shut, he would slowly put it back, at least enough to pay some bills. He didn't care if this ruined my AAA credit or that it traumatized me and left my children without lunch money. I needed to learn to trust him. And yes, he had to jerk the car on our trip home from the hospital after my cervical fusion. There were potholes all over the highway. He couldn't help that. As I sat in the recliner recovering from my cervical disk fusion, my son Brock would bring me flowers and cry for me and hold my hand. Dan would call him a sissy and would order him to do chores "NOW" to pull him from me. He would mock him relentlessly for any sweet sensitivity that he displayed. He smugly agreed that he did this because he was trying to make a man out of my sissy. The accusation that he dumped me backwards was a downright lie, according to Dan. He said the chair did dump backwards, but it was because I kicked him and pushed myself over. I did that to myself. I was in so much pain that it hurt to move my finger; how in the world could I raise my leg and kick him and push myself over? And the black and blue marks on my arms that I had pictures of? Well, I pinched myself and took pictures. I found it convenient that he failed to mention the fact that he made me destroy the evidence pictures of my bruises when he returned from one of his temporary separations. When he came home and walked into the TV room, yes, everyone would scramble to get up and leave the room. That is true. Dan said that he worked all day and when he arrived home, he watched what he wanted the rest of the night on the only TV we had and the kids have finally learned that. Dan went on and on, confidently explaining away all the incidences brought forth. Yes, he has told my kids that I'm a terrible mother, that I'm sick, that I am mentally ill, that I needed to grow up, and that I was living in the stone age. Those statements are all true, but he never abused me and never put his hands on me. "Cheryl is just hypersensitive and weak," Dan said with complete assurance.

The counselor changed the conversation and challenged Dan to take responsibility for his abusive behavior to my children and me. His whole demeanor instantly shifted from confidence, positivity, and self-assurance to accusation, excuse, and finger pointing. "She's the "sicko. Look at her. She would cause anyone to get angry. She has never had it so good since she met me. Nobody ever took care of her like I have. I am not appreciated at all. She is not submissive and she acts like such a Christian. She's crazy and needs to grow up and live in the real world. I'm telling you, I'm glad she's here; She needs it. Her and her values! She's hypersensitive and trying to make me look bad! I hope you can do something with her. I will leave again if she doesn't change and I will never come back!" He continued on with his opinions of me and kept getting angrier and angrier as I began to defend myself. He turned towards me as I spoke and responded abusively and aggressively, pointing his finger in my face, so close I had to back away. As his attack escalated and he pressed towards me and began to lean on me, I bent forward, put my hands over my ears, and started to cry. The counselor then stood up, demanded that he stop his assault, and told him that he had a serious anger problem and was abusive and no matter what I supposedly did, I did not deserve to be treated like that. The counselor and Dan got into a confrontation and he started pacing from one end of the office to the other, smacking one of his fists into the other opened hand while breathing heavily. His face turned redder every time the counselor demanded him to leave. After several repeated refusals, she threatened to call the police; Dan decided he didn't want to be arrested and he left, peeling out of the parking lot. She told me to call the police for protection and to pack and leave Dan that night. Convinced that our lives were in grave danger, she offered to help me to get in touch with all the resources to protect my children and myself. I decided against her advice and just accepted her offer to give me a ride home. This decision shows my mental state at that time. *What person in their right mind would go home after this kind of encounter?*

Frightened and unaware of the consequences of the counseling session, I cautiously entered my home. I found Dan to be in a good mood and as nice as could be, offering to order a pizza for us to enjoy together. *Are you kidding me?*

It was that night that I realized that my husband was a master manipulator and he was fully aware of the scare tactics he was using to control me. It was that night that I realized that I was in serious danger if I continued to live with Dan, but I wasn't leaving. Because he had taken all he wanted five times before, I knew that there would be nothing left in my house if I was the one to leave.

I cried out and prayed, "Lord, help me and please protect my family. I put this whole situation totally in your hands because I can't even think straight anymore. I don't know who I am, what to do, or where to turn. I feel so alone and so vulnerable. If it wasn't for my children, I wouldn't want to go on. Sometimes, Lord, I think they would be better off without me. I have messed up their lives so much. How do I continue to go on like this? What do I do? Is there a light at the end of this long, dark tunnel? Will things ever change? Tell me what to do, Lord? Do I stay or do I leave? Do I keep peace by agreeing with everything he says and does? Do I stand up for myself? Help me, Lord; please help me."

"Commit your way to the Lord; trust in him and he will do this; He will make your righteous reward shine like the dawn, your vindication like the noonday sun. Be still before the Lord and wait patiently for him; do not fret when people succeed in their ways, when they carry out their wicked schemes. Refrain from anger and turn from wrath; do not fret---it only leads to evil. For those who are evil will be destroyed, but those who hope in the Lord will inherit the land." Psalm 37:5-9 (NIV)

Since the last counseling session, I was on pins and needles all the time. I knew that he was playing a game with me. He was acting so nice, pretending to have turned over a new leaf, like he was living out a recently proclaimed "New Year's resolution." We all know how long they last! It was scary. I felt more at ease when he was mean and nasty. At least I knew that he was being himself. I was anxious and terrified for myself and for my family. I took all my important paperwork and some of my jewelry that had sentimental value and placed them in the home of my friend. I didn't sleep well, startled with every sound. I made sure that Dan would not drive or pick up my children from any school function or visit with their friends. I refused to go anywhere with him for fear he would do something to harm me; maybe push me out of a moving car, deliberately wreck, possibly drive me somewhere strange and leave me, perhaps even murder me and dump my body somewhere! As far as I was concerned, he was capable of any and every one of these acts!

"When I am afraid, I put my trust in you. In God, whose word I praise, in God I trust; and am not afraid. What can mere mortals do to me?" Psalm 56:3,4 (NIV)

Dan said that I had set him up in the counseling session. Because I had gone for weeks without him and filled her mind with lies about him, he didn't have a fair chance to tell his side of the story. And of course, a woman is going to take another woman's side.

He wanted to go to a man. We would go together so I wouldn't have the chance to tell any lies. We would go in together and each tell our side while the other was sitting there. That is the only fair way. I agreed to go to the man he picked and on his terms.

The evening came for our counseling session. We waited for a few minutes and an older distinguished man came out of an office and introduced himself to us. When he called me in first, I could feel the atmosphere grow tense as Dan stood to his feet and protested. The counselor sternly told him he wanted a few minutes with each of us and then he would talk to us together. In the few minutes I had alone, I briefly told the counselor about my life with Dan and what happened at the other counselor's office. Dan went in and had his opportunity to share and then I was called in to join him. I honestly don't remember what was said. I know we were in the office together a very short time before Dan and the counselor were shouting at each other. Dan was enraged and the counselor ordered him to leave and Dan went furiously stomping out of the office, slamming the door behind him as well as the outside door. The counselor told me that Dan will never change and bluntly said as he stared me in the eye, "Get rid of him before he hurts you and he **will** hurt you."

"Keep me as the apple of your eye; hide me in the shadow of your wings." Psalm 17:8 (NIV)

Hide Me, Lord,

in the Shadow of Your Wings

Cheryl Marie

Hide me, Lord, in the shadow of your wings;
Protect me from all the trouble this world brings.
Like a mother bird who shields her young
And keeps them from all harm,
Hide me, Lord, in the shadow of your wings.

Hide me, Lord, in the shadow of your wings.
Help me see your mighty hand
In each and every thing
That comes into my life, whether good or bad,
I'll see your presence there.

Hide me, Lord, in the shadow of your wings.

And when the storms roll in, the strong winds blow,
I'll be safe, I'll be sound.
Underneath your mighty wings,
I will lay my burdens down.

You're shielding me, protecting me,
Through all my heart will sing
For I'm hiding in the shadow of your wings.

Hide me, Lord, in the shadow of your wings.
I find comfort, I find peace in all things.
I can live each day and know that
I'm the apple of your eye.
Hide me, Lord, in the shadow of your wings

The day came when everything climaxed and my chil-dren and I escaped with our lives. Dan walked in unexpectedly one morning and I just knew in my spirit that I was in danger. Maybe it was the look in his eye or the smirk on his face. I whispered a silent thank you to God that my little ones were at school. I had gone to the bank earlier and cashed a check belonging to my children and had laid that money in an envelope on the kitchen table. He was aware that I was doing this and he knew my habit of putting it on the table. He acted suspiciously as he entered the house, attempting to greet me and ask me how my day was. I responded calmly and indifferently. He walked to the kitchen, grabbed the envelope of money and ran out the door to his car. I ran after him and hung onto the handle of the car door as he proceeded to drive down the street. There were people walking and watching the whole episode; I began yelling for him to give back my children's money. Because he always wanted to look good in front of people, I knew that he would be embarrassed. He threw the envelope of money out the car window, calling me filthy vulgar names and screaming malicious threats. I sensed a strong warning of danger. I let go of the handle, picked up the money and darted full speed for the door of the house and locked it behind me. I heard the screeching of his tires and, through the window, I saw him back up into the driveway. I called 911, blurted out my address, just as Dan unlocked the door, barged in, and ripped the phone cord out of the wall. When he realized that I may have connected for help, he threatened me as he ran back outside and sped away.

The police arrived within a few minutes and took me to a Domestic Violence Shelter and my children joined me after school. A wonderful counselor talked to me and convinced me that my children and I were in grave danger. There was no turning back; It was time to take the necessary steps to keep us safe. I was expertly guided in what I needed to do and I filed for a "Protection from Abuse" order. The police found Dan and escorted him through the house for his belongings while we were away. He took everything out of my home that he could take in one trip and he also took the car in the driveway. He had conveniently had the other car in the shop that week. I learned later that he had lied and that it was parked at the house of a fellow worker. My car, which was too small for him, was left. I was just thankful that he didn't take our lives. Stuff doesn't matter. At the shelter, my family found support and understanding. I was educated and counseled.

My dad had visited us frequently during our seven and one-half year marriage. He would come and stay for a few days at a time. Dan was always on his best behavior during these visits. It would confuse the children when he treated them like human beings. Dad didn't like Dan. He hated his bragging about himself and his "self-righteous and know-it-all attitude." Dan did not care for my father either. These visits were just an additional stress in my life, but the children enjoyed the attention their grandfather gave them.

When we were taken to the Domestic Abuse Shelter, I called my dad and he dropped everything and was at my house that same night. He changed all the locks on my doors. "Why didn't you ever tell anyone what was going on?" Dad asked. "Why did you not tell me?" He was upset. I thought he was going to be "done with me" again. I couldn't handle that right now with all I had just been through. He decided to stay with us a few weeks to protect us.

It is a proven fact that the most dangerous time for victims of domestic abuse is after the relationship is ended. We were all uneasy, even with my dad there. We had no protection and Dan was big, strong, and unpredictable. Post-traumatic stress disorder caused me to suffer from panic attacks at night. I would take hours to fall asleep only to wake up and smell his cologne. I struggled to breathe and my heart pounded with fear. I couldn't distinguish what was real and what was not. I would check the bureau to see if his clothes were there. I would check the nightstand drawer for the large sharp butcher knife that he kept there as a silent threat to do whatever he said. I would run to my children's rooms to make sure they were sleeping in their beds. Only then would I realize that he was really gone and we were safe, at least for the time being. "Lord, please watch over us and keep us in your care."

"In peace I will lie down and sleep, for you alone, Lord, make me dwell in safety." Psalm 4:8 (NIV)

"Do not be anxious about anything, but in every situation, by prayer and petition, with thanksgiving, present your requests to God. And the peace of God which transcends all understanding, will guard your hearts and your mind in Christ Jesus." Phil 4:6,7 (NIV)

Dan contested the "Protection from Abuse" order and I was called into court. I could not afford to hire a lawyer since he had totally drained me of all finances. I was appointed an attorney and my Domestic Abuse advocate from the shelter accompanied me to the courthouse, which was about a thirty-five-minute drive from my house. Dan hired the most aggressive attorney in our town and they came prepared with his folder of fabrications and deceptions. The "Protection from Abuse" order was removed by the judge after hearing the expertly presented twisted lies. As I sat in the courtroom stunned and hysterical with fear, my advocate stood and convinced the court to hold Dan there for twenty minutes after I left, to assure my safety on the highway. I hustled out quickly, shocked, sickened, and terrified for me and my children's safety. I received a call after I arrived home. When my advocate discussed my case with the judge, he confided that my attorney did not defend my case in the proper way. Even though he believed that Dan was a threat to me, based on the evidence presented, he had no option but to lift the order.

This explanation did not help me to feel any better or any safer. Instead, I became furiously angry at the whole justice system. The panic attacks worsened. I was literally sick from the horror of what could happen. Dan knew that the only way he could really destroy me was through my children. I didn't want them out of my sight, but they had to go to school and have a social life. I alerted the schools and the parents of their friends. Stress, anxiety, and apprehension consumed me.

During this time, my youngest daughter, Sheila, had to write a poem in school for her English class. This poem describes her perception of Dan so powerfully. This is what she wrote.

I Remember You

Your voice,

The kind that sends chills up your spine;

Your thunderous roar, ricocheting off the walls;

Those lying words you spoke in your sly tone,

Brainwashed by your silver tongue;

Your eyes,

They say the eyes are the window to the soul;

Your soul was apparent from the beginning.

When you looked through them you were

Blinded by deception.

Your smell,

It reeked of antagonism and belligerence;
The odor of a foul rat that can never be disguised.
A trail of your stench is everywhere you go.

Your touch,
As hard as a rock,
Adamant and inexorable,
Never to falter.
I never trusted you.
I never cared for you.
Yet, I will always remember you.

The divorce was finally granted after two long years. The total debt I was left with at the end of this horrendous nightmare was fifty-eight thousand dollars and I had nothing to show for it! In addition to that, he now owned half of my house.

I prayed for God's help and strength to be with my chil-dren and me as we attempted to rebuild our lives. *What would happen to us? Could we go on? Would I be able to meet the needs of my family?* I had been told over and over by Dan that I couldn't make it on my own, that I needed him to take care of me, I was weak and stupid, I had my head in the sand, and I wouldn't be able to survive.

"For I know the plans I have for you, declares the Lord, plans to prosper you and not to harm you, plans to give you hope

and a future. Then you will call on me and come and pray to me, and I will listen to you. You will seek me and find me when you seek me with all your heart. I will be found by you declares the Lord and will bring you back from captivity." Jeremiah 29:11-14 (NIV)

"Forget the former things; do not dwell on the past. See, I am doing a new thing! Now it springs up; do you not perceive it? I am making a way in the wilderness and streams in the waste-land." Isaiah 43:18,19 (NIV)

God had plans for my life. I would seek to do His will. He always answers prayer and is always faithful. I would make it with the Lord's help.

Please know that Dan had many good qualities, despite the bad. I remember our long talks while we were dating. He talked of the physical abuse that he suffered as a boy at the hands of his dad. I remember him crying as he told me about all the times he was brutally beaten as his mother screamed and begged his father to stop. He told me about the incident when his dad broke his arm. God loves Dan and understands the little boy that was severely punished when he failed in the eyes of his male role model. My heart reaches out to Dan or to anyone else who has suffered abuse or had their spirits crushed in this way. Hurting people hurt people. I don't dislike Dan, but I do dislike what he did to my children and I. I do regret that he refused to admit that he had a problem and to obtain the skills he needed to control his emotions. I am sorry that I waited so long to get the help I needed to escape. I sincerely forgive Dan for all the grief he caused. I believe he has a lot of pain inside and I pray the Lord will grant him the peace and healing that he desperately needs.

"If you don't heal what hurt you, you'll bleed on people who didn't cut you." Unknown

Chapter 14

Finally, Free!

Days turned into weeks, and weeks to months. I began to feel a new freedom in my single life, coming and going as I pleased, having friends, managing my household, going to church, supporting my twin girls in their athletic competitions, even eating popcorn for dinner if I wanted! After so many difficult years of living under oppression, my children and I felt like we were released from a no bars, but equally confining prison. It didn't take us long to start enjoying ourselves.

Life was good, but it was not easy. Because of Dan's spending habits, I was deep in debt with nothing to show for it. Having learned the benefits of forgiveness a long time ago, I was not going to let bitterness grow in me. Jillian had married and was busy in her new life with her husband. Sadly, Scott and Brock were no longer with me and I looked to God for the strength to go on without them. Scott, living on his own, was doing as he pleased.

Brock, living with CJ, did not have rules to follow. I couldn't change lifestyle choices they had made. I couldn't change their lives in the hands of my God. I had Sheila and Shana to raise and they gave me the motivation to put the past behind me and look forward to a brighter future. We trusted the Lord to supply all our needs. I had to deal with the never-ending pain of fibromyalgia twenty-four hours a day, but I would not give in and go to bed. I could not allow that to happen ever again. Instead, I prayed and asked the Lord to help me to deal with the relentless antagonizing pain of the disease.

"Have mercy on me, Lord, for I am faint; Heal me, Lord, for my bones are in agony." Psalm 6:2,3 (NIV)

It took a while to overcome the symptoms of post-traumatic stress disorder and to even think clearly to move for-ward. Within a few months, I decided that I was ready to start classes at a business college to earn a degree. My education was paid for by a federal program for displaced homemakers. This was a real step in faith since I had been told for so long that I was stupid, incapable of caring for myself and my children, had my head in the sand, and couldn't survive without help. I chose the most difficult course, "Information Support Systems Technology," which is troubleshooting, repairing, and networking computers. I would definitely need God's help, especially since I had never cared about or even turned on a computer! I guess I wanted to prove to the world that I wasn't dumb! But God is a God of the impossible. He was glorified when I graduated with an A- average. I now had an Associate Degree. I say that, not to give any credit to myself, but to say that with God, all things are possible.

I was hired by the same school as an Admissions Representative. I prepared power point presentations about the job market and I traveled to schools to meet with potential students. I gathered leads and did follow ups calls to set up appointments for possible admissions to the business college. What a shot in the arm for my self-esteem! I could hardly think or communicate clearly at my interview to be accepted as a student and here I was, less than two years later, with a degree in my hand and a job offer. God was restoring all that had been stripped away from me. I now had self-worth, dignity, clarity of thought, self-esteem, confidence, friends, a future, goals, and purpose. Praise the Lord!

As a student and an employee of the college, God brought women to me-women who were going through divorce or abusive relationships. I began a group at my home to support these women and to help them put their faith and trust in Jesus Christ, the answer to all their problems.

Even though I worked long hours, I enjoyed my job for almost two years. One day, sitting at a stop sign in the company van, a truck failed to stop and smashed into the rear of my vehicle. I spent the next one and one-half years recovering from a low back injury. I had no choice but to resign from my job. God answered prayer and eventually healed my back, but the fibromyalgia continued to plague me.

Sheila, Shana, and I began to travel to churches and events most weekends, singing for the Lord, averaging about ninety concerts a year. In addition to that, I was accepting invitations during the week to share my testimony in churches and various women's groups. Lives were being touched and souls were being saved as God used our broken lives for His glory!

I decided to start my own cleaning and organizing business so that I could support my family and be free to do the Lord's work when the doors opened. I enjoyed spending time with people and helping them to feel better about their homes. Having the ability to use my organizational skills and to share my faith while earning a living, was a plus. I loved teaching homeowners how to organize wisely and how to keep what they wanted without clutter. The constant movement of this type of work kept my body from becoming stiff and more painful.

I also became the music director of my church. Playing music, teaching music, arranging music, directing music, singing music; it doesn't get any better than that!

For nine years, I worked hard, most days starting early and ending late. I felt like all I did was work and sleep, but with the Lord's help, we were making it! Our days were filled, we were happy, my debt was paid, and God was blessing our little family.

Chapter 15

Visits from Dad

Dad visited often, always unannounced. He stayed for a couple of weeks and he left the same way. We woke in the morning to find him gone. I never knew when he was coming or going. This was upsetting to me because I always wondered if he was upset and that was his reason for leaving. I told him that leaving unannounced and abruptly troubled my children. They cried because they didn't get to say good-bye. Unaffected by the feelings of my kids, he continued to do it "his" way.

During his little vacation with us, he would try to tell me how to raise my children. They should be home, not going to extracurricular activities. They didn't need to be "running all the time." I wasn't raising them right. He worried about them because I was "too lenient." I let them date. I let them have their friends over too much. I let them talk on the phone. I was too strict with what they watched on TV.

Dad tried to teach me how to do things "the right way." In the car, he reprimanded me because my hands weren't at the proper place on the steering wheel. In his opinion, I had a lead foot; I should press the gas lightly "like there were eggshells underneath it." I didn't stack the dishwasher efficiently. I left too many lights on. I kept the house too cold. I used too much water. I didn't buy the right brands of food. I didn't arrive one-half hour before my appointments instead of the required fifteen minutes. On and on and on; I did nothing right.

He compared my cooking with his sister's recipes, making me feel inadequate. He preached to me about the fats and cholesterol in everything I made and monitored every ingredient in my recipes.

According to him, my life was "too busy." He could never "live like we do." I'm never home. I work too much and when I am off, I should stay home. My children were involved in too many activities.

We had all our music equipment set up in the large sunlit front room in our home at all times. We practiced several times a week. In spite of the age difference between my daughters and myself, Sheila, Shana, and I were all on the same page with our music. We chose songs that touched us and sang them with conviction. If the song did not bless us, how could we sing it from our hearts and expect it to move the audience? We were sticklers when it came to harmonies, every note perfectly blended. I hated to sing with my girls when Dad was there. He didn't care for the song; why didn't we sing songs he liked? The music was too loud, too fast, or too slow. Why did we do all genres? He liked country. It infuriated me when he couldn't understand that we weren't singing to entertain him or anyone else. We were singing what God had led us to sing in the way He impressed us to sing it. It got to the point where I refused to practice while Dad was in my home. Thank the Lord, he only attended a few concerts or services we did. I always felt like I was under a microscope being picked apart.

Every day he was at my house, he would steer the conversation and complain and criticize my mother and sisters, calling them terrible names and degrading their character. I sternly told him that I would not tolerate his disrespect of my loved ones. I would not accept his name-calling of my family in front of my children and me. I would not listen to his twisted thinking and outrageous accusations. He knew where I stood and that I was not in support of his behavior. I told him he was wrong to reject and disown thirteen-year old Rose when he and my mom separated. She was a child! It was also wrong to do the same with my other sisters. I felt guilty for even having a relationship with him because of the pain he inflicted on my siblings. My comments made him think about what he had done to Rose. "Fine," he said. "You bring her here and take her into your front room and I will be here in the family room. You stand in the hallway between the rooms and ask her the questions I have and then you tell me what she answers." "I will not! You have done this to me all my life! I will not support your grudge and bitterness to my sister. She was just an innocent child and you have not spoken to her in twenty-four years!" I cried. He had no intention of making things right. I would not take part in his plan to further degrade and cause pain to her already wounded heart. This is the way I grew up and I wasn't going there again. I was an adult, he was in my home, and I would not jump through his hoops.

He complained about his own sisters and brothers. I heard all that he didn't like about them. I told him that he needed to release his resentment, anger, bitterness, and unforgiveness because it was destroying him.

Everything had to be done "his" way. His warped views and perspectives were the only way to see things. In his eyes, everyone was wrong and he was right.

Dad did not like that I wouldn't change my life to suit him. No one had ever stood up to him. He began to voice his frustration to Jillian, CJ, and his sisters and brothers. His frequent visits to Jillian's to criticize me as a mother and a person infuriated me. What in the world was he telling them? I felt like I couldn't face my child because of the perverted conversations he shared with them. His discussions about my life with my ex-husband, CJ, were totally inappropriate. I felt like I couldn't even face my aunts and uncles on his side of the family because of the stories he may have told them from his distorted perspective. What were they believing about me?

One day when he was visiting, he and my girls were playing a game at the kitchen table. My landline was in the kitchen also. I answered the ringing phone and proceeded to stretch the flexible cord to another room so I would be able to hear better. After I hung up the phone and returned to the noisy kitchen, my father said, "What do you have to hide?" "What are you talking about?" I asked. "Well, you went in the other room to talk on the phone so I couldn't hear your conversation. Your mother always did that when she talked to men. What are you hiding? You were on a long time. What were you saying about me?" I was in shock. Really? Did I hear him correctly? I could feel the anger rising within me and I took a moment to calm myself before I spoke. "Dad, this is my house and my phone and I can talk to whoever I want to wherever I want to as long as I want. My conversation had nothing to do with you. If you want to be upset, go ahead, but you won't get an apology from me. I did nothing wrong." I walked out of the room and went upstairs to cool down. To my surprise, he talked to me the next morning.

During the years he visited us, he repaired anything in the house that needed attention. I never had to buy new if something broke because Dad would fix it. He was a brilliant man. He was glad to come to our aid and we were thankful for his assistance. He showed his love in this way. Dad also helped us out financially. He paid for piano lessons for Shana and Sheila. Occasionally, he put some money on the table when he left if he knew we had a specific need. I so appreciated his support. Because he did so much for us, I always felt like I had to tolerate his behavior. I was in turmoil all the time because I couldn't keep my mouth shut when I heard the remarks and slurs against my loved ones. I defended them and then felt guilty because he took care of us so well in so many ways.

I love my dad, but his visits drained me. It took me some time to realize that I had so much anger toward him from my childhood and it was compounded by his unchanged behavior toward me as an adult.

Fourteen years ago, my father chose to stop speaking to me again for some unknown reason and has walked not only out of my life, but also the lives of all my children and grandchildren. He left me a note that said he was "done with us for life." I have tried to mend this relationship many times. I have sent cards. I have sent gifts. Each package is returned, unopened, with "REFUSED" scribbled across the front. Each time I am hurt again by his rejection and his unwillingness to even tell me what I did. The pain has the same effect as it did when I was a little girl and it hurts so deeply.

A Letter to Dad

Cheryl Marie

My heart is torn, it's been too long;
It doesn't matter who's right or wrong.
I miss your smile; I miss your touch;
I want too make it right so much.

We're family, oh can't you see?
I belong to you; you belong to me.
My children cry and I cry, too.
I want to spend some time with you.

So many days, you've not been here.
I wonder if you even care.
You left my life with a hardened heart;
Decided that our paths must part.
No reason-you just walked away
What did I do? What did I say?

Time is precious-it goes too fast;
Let's forgive, forget the past.

Begging to Die

Sheila, Shana and I were in Nashville, Tennessee for a week of musical training for our ministry. Walking across a parking lot, a searing pain went through my left knee and I nearly collapsed onto the pavement. The girls had to drive the long trip home and after a doctor's visit, I learned that both my knees would eventually need replaced. On crutches, I had to rely on friends to take me back and forth to my doctor, seventy-five miles away, to receive a series of shots in my left knee. When these shots gave me no relief, I had to continue making these trips to receive gel injections in the same knee. Treatments lasted nearly a year and the twins had to help me with my cleaning/organizing business. They already carried a full load in college. The treatments failed to relieve the pain so I was scheduled for arthroscopic surgery.

I had my left knee done and I recovered well, but the pain remained. A replacement was needed, but the insurance would not pay for it until I received the shots, the gel injections, and the arthroscopic surgery.

A few months later, the process started all over again and I had to endure all the visits for shots and gel injections in my right knee. After several months of treatment, arthroscopic surgery was scheduled.

I was the first patient scheduled in surgery that day. The pain from the fibromyalgia was causing my blood pressure to spike. I had to wait all day for my blood pressure to come down to an acceptable level before they could proceed with the surgery. Finally, it was my turn. Mine would be the last operation of the day, but the surgeon was nowhere to be found. I was getting anxious and the nurses made excuses for him. After what seemed like hours, the doctor was located and they took me to the operating room. After I was awake and was coherent, my friend and I began the seventy-five-mile trip home.

Even though I stayed off the knee or used crutches, the pain increased. I tolerated the escalating discomfort by taking pain medication. I noticed that I had a very wide black and blue bruise above my right knee that went all around my leg, but I didn't think much of it at the time.

Christmas was three days after the surgery. Sheila, Shana and I went to Jillian's house for dinner. It took everything in me to even sit there without moaning because of the intensity of the pain. I couldn't eat any of the delicious Christmas meal my daughter prepared. That night the nightmare began.

The pain became so horrific that I was incoherent. I have never experienced pain like that before. I pray I will never experience pain like that again! The most intense labor during childbirth was no comparison to this pain. Within a few days, my mom came to take care of me. The first night she stayed, she found me on the floor, huddled in a corner of my bedroom rolled up in an afghan, swaying back and forth, out of my mind, sobbing in agony. After that, she literally stayed by my side day and night. It amazes me how she had the strength to watch her child go through what I did. She was a rock. Just knowing Mom was there was comforting, but there was nothing she could do to relieve my intense and endless suffering, except to make sure that I had the right amount of pain medication at the designated time. She was also careful to keep it out of my reach because I would have taken the whole bottle without a second thought.

There was absolutely nothing that anyone could do. I was now in a wheelchair, unable to walk. I was taken to emergency rooms, admitted to hospitals for observation, to pain clinics, and doctor's offices in my city and the cities nearby. I saw general practitioners, orthopedic surgeons, neurologists, and physical therapists. Each was stumped. I was given narcotics to take by mouth and pain patches to wear, but the horrendous throbbing could not be controlled. My days and nights ran together. I screamed, cried, and moaned deliriously for the next two weeks with the excruciating pain. I wanted to die. I begged the Lord to have mercy on me and take me home. Those were the only words that I knew how to pray.

"In the same way, the Spirit helps us in our weakness. We do not know what we ought to pray for, but the Spirit himself intercedes for us through wordless groans. And he who searches

our hearts knows the mind of the Spirit, because the Spirit intercedes for God's people in accordance with the will of God." **Romans 8:26,27 (NIV)**

I was pumped with strong narcotics and incapable of thinking beyond the dreadful pain. My mom and my children had to make all my health decisions for me.

After some medical counsel, all agreed that I would be taken to a hospital several hours away for admittance. My family was advised to take me to the emergency room and to let them assess my condition with hopes of a decision to keep me. I had not eaten for over two weeks. I was dehydrated because I only sipped enough water to take medication. Several attempts had been made for MRI scans of different parts of my body, but because of my pain level, I could not lie still for the length of time needed to complete the tests. If I were to be admitted, I could be anesthetized and all the evaluations and testing could be done at the same time. My blood pressure was soaring because of the horrendous pain. I was mentally and physically unable to care for myself and so far, no one could figure out how to help me.

My stay in the hospital was the worst. It was like a bad dream from which you couldn't wake. I was admitted and taken to a floor in the facility that was used as an overflow area. The rooms were filled with patients with all types of maladies with all levels of severity. Not knowing this at first, my loved ones were just thrilled to have me under constant professional care with the hope of getting to the root cause of all the agonizing pain. As the events unfolded, the relief they felt having me in the medical facility turned into extreme stress and the hope turned into recurring disappointment and despair.

The interior of this wing on this particular floor of the building reminded me of a hospital in the 1940's or 1950's. Everything seemed to be in black and white. The corridors and rooms were disgustingly dirty, old, dark and gloomy. The air was musty, stale and stagnant, almost thick enough to see smog-like clouds of grey. The atmosphere was one of heaviness instead of cheer. The staff scurried about like wind-up robots, seemingly overworked, unfriendly and uncaring.

I remember feeling like I was unimportant and a nui-sance as I was, callously and insensitively, placed in a room with young lady who looked like she was in her early twenties. Since I drifted in and out of consciousness, I am unable to accurately record time sequences, but I will tell my story to the best of my ability. One day as the nurse was in our room, I overheard the conversation between her and this young woman. Even though I was medicated heavily, I realized that I was sharing the room with a patient who had a highly communicable incurable disease. My hospital gown had a small pocket on the top front of it, right smack in the middle, where I kept my cell phone. It was comforting to have the phone right near my heart. That allowed me to easily connect to my family who were about two-and one-half hours away. I called Jillian and whispered what I had overheard and she assured me that she would take care of the situation.

The following morning, the staff treated me with cold indifference as they moved me. I remember thinking, *I know I am really out of it, but a smile and some kind words would really be nice right now!* Instead I was rolled out of the room quickly and jerked around the corners like I was a cart of supplies and my bed was placed into the empty spot in my new destination. Without comment, the staff disappeared once again. This room was larger and seemed to be a little better. The woman in the bed beside mine was much closer to my age and was trying to engage me in conversation even as they wheeled me in. She asked me if I wanted to watch TV with her. "No, not now," I moaned. Ignoring my answer, she clicked on the TV and turned up the volume until it was blaring. Shouting in an earsplitting voice, she searched through the channels and demanded to know what station I wanted to watch. I thought to myself, *Are you serious? Can you not see that I don't feel like a pajama party!* I don't ever remember being so sick. I couldn't hold my eyes open; I was extremely dizzy, I was violently vomiting from the pain medication that was pumped into my veins, and the throbbing in my leg was unbearable. When she realized that I wasn't going to watch TV with her, she called someone on her phone. That's when I realized I wasn't dealing with a woman with a complete understanding of her behavior. Her voice was nasty, crude, and piercing enough to be heard outside our room with the door closed. From what I can remember, she talked about what everyone had done to her to put her in the hospital and of her planned revenge. She used very foul language and made statements that assured me that she was not in a stable mental state. Soon her conversation shifted to me. She said I was rude because I wouldn't talk to her or watch TV with her. She was going to take care of me and make me wish I had been nicer to her! I was in danger and I was helpless to defend myself. I was in so much misery and so ill that I couldn't tolerate the threatening atmosphere. I reached for my handy cell phone next to my heart and I called my daughter. The only thing I could say frantically under my breath was, "Get me out of here; right now! Get me out of here!" Jillian must have called the nurse's station and within a few minutes, I was wheeled out into the hallway where I laid for the rest of the day. They told my roommate that I was going for tests when she demanded to know where they were taking me.

After ten to twelve hours of lying alone in the hallway, a couple of adjustments to my IV, and a few inattentive glances in passing, I was taken to another room on the same gruesome floor. It was late evening and the curtain was pulled, the lights were out and I was left alone in the darkness. The next morning, I woke to find a very nice, friendly young woman in the next bed who immediately asked me what happened to me. She commented that I moaned and cried all night long. She proceeded to share that she is in the hospital every other week or so due to her condition. They stabilize her and after a few days, they send her back home. As she explained in more detail, I thought to myself, *Am I dreaming; is this a nightmare? She has a highly communicable, incurable disease also!* I reached for my cell phone as soon as my roommate went into the bathroom and I again called Jillian. She was very disturbed and said that she would leave immediately and take the two and one-half hour trip down. She assured me all would be ok. By early evening, Jillian had spoken with every hospital official that she could and I was moved once more to another dark, gloomy room. This time, my daughter gave her approval before she left the hospital. The pain had not improved and the stress was monumental! *Lord, just end this nightmare and take me home with you!*

Several of my friends from church and my pastor want-ed to come to see me, but I refused any phone calls or visitors except Jillian or my mother. I was just too sick to be social. I asked Sheila and Shana not to come. They were in college at the time and I wanted them to concentrate on their studies and their work commitments. Everyday Mom walked, in the dead of winter, to the bus stop near her home; she boarded a crowded bus for the forty-five-minute trip and walked, in the wind and snow, up a steep hill to the hospital. After sitting at the foot of my bed as I slept all day, she walked back down that hill and waited for a bus to take her home. She did this for twenty-one days while I was in the hospital. She was eighty years old at the time! I remember feeling so bad because when she came, I couldn't even talk to her. Sitting and watching me suffer all day every day was not a good thing for her to do, but I couldn't stop her from coming. This commitment to me helped heal years of disturbing, hurtful memories. A little love goes a long way, and I love her and appreciate her for seeing me through this horrible time in my life.

I begged and pleaded to God over and over to let me die. I endured grueling tests while I was in misery with the debilitating pain. I couldn't eat and had to be fed intravenously. I had severe stomach spasms. I vomited constantly from the med-ication. I was extremely weak. No one answered our questions. When my mom questioned the nurses, they said they had to talk to the doctor. When she questioned the doctor, he said he had to discuss it with another doctor. Jillian could not get any answers on her calls either. Everyone seemed to avoid the diagnosis or any explanation of my incapacitating pain.

One day, while lying on a gurney waiting for a test, a woman passed me as she was being pushed in a wheelchair. She pointed at me and started yelling that she was going to kill me for moving out of her room. Even though I was heavily drugged, fear overcame me because I was lying there alone and helpless. Nurses swiftly came to my rescue and wheeled me down the hall and she was quickly taken in another direction. The whole episode lasted less than a minute, but my heart pounded for a long time after that! The screaming woman was my former roommate. She was being released; I would be safe! I thank God for giving me the sense that I was in danger that day in her room. In spite of the grogginess from the medications, I was prompted by the Lord to call my daughter for help. Who knows what may have happened to me without His divine intervention?

"Blessed are those who have regard for the weak; the Lord delivers them in times of trouble. The Lord protects and preserves them; they are counted among the blessed in the land--he does not give them over to the desire of their foes. The Lord sustains them on their sickbed and restores them from their bed of illness." *Psalm 41:1-3 (NIV)*

On the morning of the twenty-first day of my hospital stay, a nurse walked into my room and announced, very coldly, that I was to be released. "Did I hear you correctly? I am no better than I was the day I was admitted," I asked. She avoided my question when I asked her about my diagnosis and told me that I would have to talk to my doctor on my follow-up visit in about a week. I was so shocked that I had a hard time deciphering what she had just told me and my thoughts were confusing to me. Let me understand this correctly; *I am being discharged in the same condition that I was when admitted twenty-one days ago with no diagnosis?* Another call was made to Jillian and in spite of her protests, I was leaving that day with no relief and no answers. Anyone with any brains at all could see that I was in no condition to be released. The pain was still horrible and I still had no idea of the cause. On such short notice, none of my daughters could make the drive to take me home. I called my pastor and he and my friend, Bill, made the long trip to pick me up and drive me back home.

Mom made arrangements to come and stay again to be my twenty-four hour a day nurse. My medication was increased until it began to take the edge off the sharpness of the pain. The high dosages of several narcotics and a strong pain patch caused me to be groggier, more unstable, and more incapable of doing much of anything without assistance. I couldn't eat and lost a considerable amount of weight. One of the things I remember is Mom being right beside me in my big queen bed every time I opened my eyes, whether it was day or night.

When I returned for a follow-up visit, the neurologist, upon examination saw that I had not improved. I was in a wheelchair, unable to even stand alone. My right leg was considerably weaker than my left leg. The narcotics were not completely controlling the pain. He chose his words carefully when my girls and I questioned him about what was wrong with me. He had thought at first that I had a problem with my back and all those horrible tests had revealed that my back was not the problem. I pressed him for a diagnosis. Finally, he reluctantly told me that the tourniquet, that was put on my leg over a month before to have the arthroscopic surgery on my right knee, must have been too tight and had permanently crushed both the obturator and femoral nerves. *That explains the black and blue mark that circled my leg!* These are the main nerves in the leg and they could not be repaired. They would not heal, and I would be on medication to control pain for the rest of my life. The doctor quickly added, very adamantly, that if I were to legally pursue this medical mistake, he would deny everything he just told me.

The coldness and lack of empathy in his voice caused a surge of anger to rise within me. I felt heat rushing through my body and my heart began to pound. Even in my sitting position, I found it very difficult to hold myself upright from the weakness and dizziness that seemed to engulf me. In spite of the fact that my thinking was very impaired from the pain medication, I understood enough to know that I had suffered tremendously and needlessly. The medical personnel at the hospital knew that it was the tourniquet and were trying to figure out a way to cover it up. That is why they treated me so coldly. I was put through all the grueling tests to try to find something else to blame it on! That's why they never told me the results of all the unnecessary tests! Flashbacks of my unbearable hospital stay raced through my mind. I recalled the day before I was told to leave, when I had an EMG nerve test done on both of my legs. I cried and screamed, delirious with pain. I couldn't lie still; I couldn't answer the technician's questions. I felt helpless as I endured the painful tests. The doctor was consulted because of the abnormality of the findings. He then repeated the extremely painful tests and reported to me that I had severe nerve damage in my right leg. I was in such a bad state that I had forgotten about it. That was the reason they abruptly discharged me the very next morning. They probably hoped the true diagnosis would never surface. *How could they do something like this to someone? How cold and callous! No, Lord. Please, Lord; I can't live like this! Have mercy on me, Father. I have no strength left. How could this happen? What do I do now? How can I work? How can I take care of my family? I just want to die. Please, just take me home! Please just let me die.*

All these questions resonated through my mind like echoes. I didn't know how I could endure the pain much longer!

My hope was gone. Death seemed to be my only option. I knew I would be with Jesus.

Chapter 17

My Angels

Thank God for a caring mother, wonderful daughters, and good friends. God blessed me with people in my life who are sensitive to other's needs. My mom was my angel during this crisis. She never left my side, day or night. My family's wisdom to make the decisions regarding my care came from the Lord. As each medical professional shrugged his shoulders, my mom and children didn't give up. They wouldn't stop until someone could give them answers. Now we had the diagnosis, I was home, and I was helpless. My girls and my mom continued to do all they could to support my needs. My friend, Bill, had stepped in when I had returned home from the hospital. He shoveled snow from my sidewalks and took care of whatever needed done at my house. Mom continued to nurse me back to health. After a month had passed, I regained enough of my strength to use a walker at home. Since my stability was hindered, I spent most of the time in bed. Repeatedly, my medication was adjusted to where the pain was tolerable (I wasn't crying) and I worked on getting back my life.

Because I was our only source of income, a month later I had to return to the finance office, where I worked as a sales representative. Restricted from driving because of all the medication, Bill drove me every day and picked me up every evening. He was there to talk about all my frustrations of my day. I had a difficult time performing my job because it required long hours, skilled sales tactics, mental endurance, and the requirement to meet next to impossible goals. I didn't have the strength for the long hours and my sales techniques were all jumbled in my groggy head. I just couldn't focus enough to try to meet the difficult goals. My boss was cold and indifferent to my pain and the effects of the narcotics on my job performance. My days were stressful and very taxing. Many nights, Bill would just listen as I went on and on about my struggles to do my work. He was my sounding board at a much-needed time in my life. *Sometimes he even took me to dinner. What a great friend!*

Chapter 18

Coincidence or Destiny

Jillian repeatedly told me that Bill was worried about me. When I was in the hospital, he stopped by for daily reports on my condition. She, Sheila and Shana thought he liked me and wanted to be more than friends. I laughed because I had known Bill for at least twenty-five years. In the past, we attended the same church. We both left that church. Here we were, years later, going to the same church again. I was the music director and Bill joined one of the ensembles. He was married at the time and I was single. We were friends. Nothing more.

A year before this very trying time in my life, my ex-husband, CJ, passed away. He had suffered for over two years with Stage Four Glioblastoma, a very aggressive brain cancer. Bill's wife had experienced a severe stroke and had also gone to her heavenly home on the same day in the same year as CJ. It was a very hard time for both our families.

My twins, Shana and Sheila, were twenty-one years old. We were actively singing concerts up until the time of my nerve injury. Our Christian music group was scheduled to sing on a gospel cruise just a couple months after my release from the hospital. We had been presenting the cruise to everyone we knew for over six months. The more people we booked to go on the cruise with us, the less money we paid for our reservation. A few family members and a group of friends from church were going. Bill, his daughter and son-in-law were excited to travel with us. Even though I was still not well, I was part of a trio with my girls and I didn't want to let them down. Sheila and Shana had been counting the days with great anticipation. Since I was trying to get my life back, I decided that I would try to go. It would be difficult for all of us because I was still in a lot of pain and confined to a wheelchair and they would have to take care of me.

We checked our bags and they wheeled me to the plane. Our flight was good and we arrived safely. My girls pushed me to the ship and we found our cabin. They were excited and were enjoying the adventure. I just wanted to rest. The pain was at a very uncomfortable level. The medication made me feel woozy and unable to think clearly.

The first concert was that evening. My daughters helped me to get ready and wheeled me to the large hall where everyone was gathered. Our friends had all come and we sat together and listened to the other musicians until it was time for us to go to the stage. My friend, Bill, wheeled me to the front, helped me out of my wheelchair, and positioned me behind the microphone stand where I could hold on. We did our portion of the program and he was right there to help me into my wheelchair. Bill sat with me for the rest of the concert that night and then wheeled me back to my cabin. He told me that he had asked his daughter and son-in-law if they would mind if he would take care of me that week since I was in a wheelchair. That would free up my girls to enjoy themselves with their boyfriends. Bill's daughter and her husband unselfishly agreed. What a great friend!

Just about every day from breakfast to bedtime, Bill pushed my wheelchair to and from all the activities on and off the ship and to the concerts each night. I don't remember very much about the cruise at all except that he was unselfishly kind, compassionate, empathetic, and faithful to his volunteer duties.

Chapter 19

Not Interested

I proclaimed, "I will never get married again unless God personally speaks to me and drops a man from Heaven right in front of me!" Those who knew me best had listened to me say that statement over and over for the past nine years. Marriage was not in my plans. I was happy single. I wasn't looking for a mate.

I didn't trust my choices in men. I had made mistakes that had not only affected myself, but also my children. I vowed that my goal was to raise my twin girls to adulthood before I even thought about my life and where it was going.

We were a happy family and I didn't want to jeopardize that happiness. The Lord had been faithful. We all had grown in our faith. Our house was peaceful. Our ministry was successful and fulfilling.

My oldest daughter, Jillian, had tried to play matchmaker with many prospective men for the last nine years. I had no interest. I had been burned so many times. For the past year, she had dropped hints on many occasions, informing me that Bill would be such a good catch and he would treat me like a queen. He was a good guy, a true Christian. Yes, he was, but he was my friend, for crying out loud!

All three girls took notice that after my nerve injury, Bill was with me every free moment and he helped me with anything and everything. They would say, "Bill likes you more than a friend and if you don't feel the same way, you need to tell him so he doesn't get hurt." I would laugh and say, "We're just friends, that's all."

Chapter 20

Man dropped from Heaven

After a long winter and chilly spring, the month of May brought warm weather and sunshine. I was still on narcotics and "my friend" had been faithful to me, helped me in many ways and drove me back and forth to work. How could you not help falling in love with such a selfless and caring person?

On May twenty third, I stood at the altar with Bill by my side. Jillian, Sheila, Shana, and Bill's daughter, Kay, surrounded us. Most of our grandchildren, my mom, sisters and closest friends all came to celebrate our marriage. I thought I needed to pinch myself to see if this was really happening. My twins beautifully sang to us. Jillian, who is a professional photographer, took our pictures and also made my bouquet with flowers from Bill's beautiful and well cared for flower garden. A wonderful catered meal was waiting at my house. There was laughter and fun until Sheila's long blonde hair caught on fire as she leaned over one of the lighted candles.

Everyone at her table jumped to her rescue and extinguished the fire. All turned out well and the day puts a smile on our face and is a sweet memory to us now. I always tease Bill that I married him because I was on drugs!

Bill definitely was the man dropped from Heaven. I had never met anyone so kind, so caring, and so devoted. We were a perfect match. We liked the same music and we both were very active. Conservative in our views, we both felt the same about finances and agreed on all life's important matters. Equally neat, we both liked a clean house and hated clutter. We loved our families, were homebodies and desired a loving and peaceful atmosphere. More importantly than anything, we were both mature Christians. Bill always said, "When you get married, your mate comes first, not yourself." No wonder I fell in love with him and his wonderful servant's heart. I was treated with such respect and dignity. He cared for me in every way just because he loved me. I never experienced that in my whole life. My past relationships were not like this one. Pain and heartache were the story of my life. I never wanted to be married again, until God dropped Bill right in front of me when I least expected it. He definitely knew what He was doing.

When Bill and I had talked about where we would live, we had discussed selling both houses and buying a home that we chose just for us. We also discussed moving into the beautiful, well-built, forty-eight hundred square foot Victorian residence that I owned. Our third possibility was me moving into his home which was about one third the size of mine.

After discussing our options, we decided that we really didn't want the hassle of finding a new home. Each of our properties was adequate. We needed to decide which to call home.

Chapter 21

A Walk Down Memory Lane

CJ and I were house hunting after the birth of Shana and Sheila. Our family had outgrown our little three-bedroom country dwelling. I had always dreamed of living in a large Victorian style home someday, but never believed it would happen. As we searched for and found suitable properties to view, nothing seemed adequate for our needs at a price we could afford. Our real estate agent knew me and my love of big old houses and she told me about one in our town. The price was twenty thousand dollars more than we could afford, but why not just look at it, just for fun? We had been praying for direction in finding our next home and as we approached this house, I whispered a prayer for His guidance. As we entered the side door, one could go down about ten steps to the basement or up about five steps to the main living area. We proceeded to the finished lower level, which consisted of a huge recreational type room, a bath, and a large laundry area, plus several storage areas. We continued to the main level which included a large foyer, living room, dining area, a kitchen, family room, and a powder room. Then we went to the upstairs five bedrooms, large foyer, and a bath. Last, to the finished attic with two more gigantic bedrooms and two large walk-in closets. The woodwork in the home was original and was a mixture of cherry and oak and included two beautiful pocket doors. Thick carpeting throughout the home was vacuumed in straight lines as if no one had ever walked on it. Stained glass windows set above the downstairs two huge picture windows added to the charm of the 1913 Victorian home. Needless to say, I was in love, but I knew that we could not afford this house. I was truly okay with that, but as we went down the five steps to leave, I glanced down to the lower level and that's when I heard this still small voice. "This is going to be your house, Cheryl, and you will open a daycare in that lower level." With five children, I had never entertained the thought of having a daycare! I was stunned and dared not say anything until God and I talked about this in more detail! I told the Lord that I loved it, but I would be happy wherever we could afford. In spite of this conversation, I just kept feeling that this was our house. After a few days, I told CJ what God was impressing on my heart and he laughed at me and told me to forget it. As I persisted in my belief that we would someday own that residence, I asked him to give an offer of twenty thousand dollars under the asking price. CJ thought that was absurd and refused to do it. I continued to pray and told CJ that I was going to give them the offer if he didn't want to "make a fool of himself." He told me to go ahead and that I was "crazy." I boldly called my agent and told her of my offer and she reluctantly said she would ask the owners. "There! I did it! Lord, I stepped out in faith and if this is to be, then so be it!" I whispered. I waited patiently and a few days later, we received the phone call that our offer was refused! "Oh well, Lord. I must have heard you wrong, but that's ok, Lord, whatever you have for us, I will be content." CJ threw it up in my face that I was "out of my mind" offering twenty thousand dollars less! Months passed and I endured the razzing from CJ and how I was so wrong and he was embarrassed that I offered such a ridiculous price. We continued to look at other properties, but I still felt deep in my heart that I had heard from the Lord correctly. I kept this to myself and had an open mind as we shopped for a new place to live. We found absolutely nothing and this only strengthened my faith that we would somehow own my Victorian dream house. A long six months passed since my offer. One day my real estate agent called and told me the wonderful news that the owners had accepted my offer! God had given us a miracle! He not only supplies our needs, but gives us the desires of our heart!

I have beautiful memories of holidays with all my family and extended family. Christmas mornings, watching my children come down the stairway with wide eyes, is a picture in my mind I will never forget.

Several years on New Year's Eve, we hosted a party with all our family and friends. Sometimes entertaining forty people, each large room in the downstairs of my home would be filled with sounds of laughter as young and old alike played games and shared stories. We would sometimes have twenty-eight overnight guests. The older crowd, parents and grandparents, stayed in the comfort of our spacious five bedrooms. Children would camp out in the large playroom downstairs. Teenage cousins would gather in the finished attic, with two extra bedrooms, and stay up most of the night. All the younger aunts and uncles slept in sleeping bags laid out beside each other through the large living and dining rooms. The only drawback was a cold shower if you were not an early riser.

We would hide our children's baskets and they would go on a whole house hunt to find them on Easter morning. Sometimes it took so long that we had to postpone the hunt until after church.

Birthday parties with little friends staying overnight were a tradition in our home. Each year I baked and decorated a cake for each of my children. This tradition started when Jillian was born and continued over the next thirty years until my youngest children, the twins were eighteen years old. The three girls usually chose themes such as "Big Bird," "Little Mermaid," "Gymnastics," "Unicorn." or "Music." My two sons would choose themes such as "Cookie Monster," "Trains," "Mickey Mouse," or "Dinosaurs

My home was full of wonderful memories of my children growing up. I enjoyed painting, wallpapering, and decorating each of my children's bedrooms especially for them. I enjoyed cooking their favorite meals and baking cookies and making candy. Jillian would have parties on Friday evenings in our finished basement. The teens would gather together, play music, eat, talk, have fun for several hours. They would clean up after themselves and be out by eleven o'clock. I enjoyed having them and was thankful that we had a place we could accommodate the friends of our children. Watching movies, eating popcorn, cuddling on the couch, listening to my twins playing the piano are some of my favorite memories. As the years flew by and the youngest grew, their friends who called me "Mom" would walk in with their sleeping bags and suitcase and announce that they were staying while their parents went on vacation. On weekends, a group of young people would gather in the family room to play games and watch TV or movies. More often than not, I would come downstairs in the morning to find someone sleeping on our couch.

When we purchased the home, I promised God that I would use it for the Lord in any way I could. On Sundays and holidays, we always had more than enough room for guests. My sister once said, "Everyone knows where you live; it is the house with the sign outside that says COME ON IN AND EAT!" My family always invited someone who needed a place to celebrate a holiday. We never wanted anyone to eat alone on a special day. One Thanksgiving, I entertained thirty-four guests. I always said our home had a revolving door. Friends of mine knew they could come and ring our doorbell any time of the day or night if they needed someone to talk to or a place to stay.

Just as the Lord had impressed on my heart, I opened a daycare in the finished basement of my home. There, my friend and I cared for many children. Loving them as my own, I enjoyed influencing their lives. Parents were pleasingly surprised with their little one's table manners, their "please and thank yous," and the responses of "Yes Ma'am." We read stories, played games, sang songs, did crafts, and learned about Jesus. We celebrated birthdays and holidays and shared our thoughts. We laughed and cried and learned respect. Feeling like a ministry to me, this daycare was an opportunity to share Christ with these little ones. Children are so special and they absorb information like a sponge. There is so much to teach them in their early years when they are so open to learning. I have so many funny stories of happenings in the daycare. Even though it can be stressful, it was a wonderful and rewarding job!

But in this same home, I also had many depressing and heartbreaking memories. I spent many nights on my couch weeping for my marriage to CJ. Even though he and my children were upstairs sleeping, I felt so abandoned and sad. I needed a partner. CJ just didn't give our marriage any priority in his life. Frustration and loneliness stole my sleep and I would go downstairs and cry, sometimes all night long.

I remember the last Christmas spent in the house as a family. I had decided months before that, after the holidays, I would tell CJ that I couldn't go on like this any longer. Our marriage was over. It was so difficult celebrating the holidays knowing that it would be the last as a family and I was the only one who knew it at the time. I was very upset, but trying to make everything memorable for my children. The decorations were hung, the presents were wrapped and hidden. I had decorated the tree alone, as I had done for many years. After everyone was in bed, I lit the lights to make sure that everything worked. As I sat there staring at it, mesmerized by the twinkling lights, I reminisced of past holidays, of memories with my children. How many years I sat just like that, all by myself, feeling so all alone. Each year hurt more than the last. Each year brought no improvement to our shattered relationship. Each year, CJ and I grew further and further apart. Yes, I would go through with the divorce. I had to. I went to bed very late and was the first one up in the morning. I proceeded down the stairs and clicked on the lights and there was the eight-foot tree with six hundred twinkling lights, a few hundred glass bulbs, and several thousand carefully hung icicles sprawled on the floor of our large living room. It was ruined, destroyed, demolished, unable to be put back together. I wept bitterly because the tree was damaged beyond repair just as my marriage and life as I knew it. I cleaned up the mess, reconstructed the tree and sadly wished that I could have done the same for my marriage. A few weeks later, Christmas came; I celebrated the birth of Jesus Christ and I silently mourned for the death of my marriage and the pain it would cause my precious children. I felt so sad and so alone, but I had no other choice.

Sights and sounds of all the abuse of my second marriage echoed through the large rooms in my home. Everywhere I looked, I saw flashbacks of horrible memories. I saw myself running from Dan. I saw me crouching in the corner in a fetal position. I saw images of my children's helpless faces with tears running down their cheeks. I heard the echoes of the horrible yelling, the crashing of furniture, the crunching of the wallboard, the splitting of wooden doorframes, the slamming of doors, the gasps of my heavy breathing and crying. Visions of bloody lips and torn shirts haunted me. A traumatic event would flash before me and the emotions I felt when it happened would well up inside me once again. When I lived there, these flashbacks were a part of my life and I tried to ignore them. As I talked about the house and these feelings with Bill, I would still experience the emotions attached to the events.

Even though it was a home that I had prayed for and once loved, a home where I raised my children, a home that was a refuge for those who needed help or a good meal, a home where family and friends made great memories together, a home of quality and beauty, Bill and I decided that this was one place we didn't want to live.

After a short quiet honeymoon, we settled into married life. We were so well matched by God that relocating to Bill's home seemed natural and I had a sense that it was home from the minute I walked in.

Sheila and Shana, who were now in their twenties, could stay in the large home that I owned. The house would be put up for sale in the spring of the following year. The girls would have time to find apartments and make the transition to life on their own.

Chapter 22

Life with Bill

Bill was a secure, quiet and laid-back kind of man and was always on an even keel. His home reflected his personality. Before we started our relationship, he had painted the bedroom a light shade of tan, liked it so much that he continued to paint every room in the house with the same paint. All the rugs were tan. The draperies were tan. The furniture was tan and brown. The walls in all the rooms were bare. There were no pictures, nick knacks or plants. The house was spotlessly clean and Bill was content.

I love vibrant color and pictures on walls and decorated windows. I love my special treasures and portraits displayed. I love plants. I love wallpaper. This was quite a contrast in decorating styles. We decided that I would move into Bill's home after our marriage. He promised I could make this home my own with my unique style of decorating. He thought that was reasonable. Our living arrangements were agreed upon, but I'm not sure he really knew what that meant at the time!

Even though I made my living as a professional organizer, Sheila says that I am an organized hoarder. That is not totally the way I see it. I am very sentimental and I saved pictures and homemade gifts from my five children in totes marked "Precious Gifts from My Children." I also have a tote of the homemade gifts from myself to my beloved grandmother. I have totes for everything I keep. For example, one for craft supplies, one for small antiques, one for picture frames, one for material, one for silk flowers. I also have about ten totes for Christmas decorations, three for Easter, two for the Fourth of July. I have three for Styrofoam plates, cups, and plastic ware, one with gift boxes and bags, and one with bows and ribbon. All year I shop for bargains for all my loved ones and store them in totes with each family's name. I am usually done with my Christmas shopping by September or October. Each tote is the same color and brand and each is labeled accordingly. My children make fun of me, but whenever they are in need of anything, they come to me because they know I probably have a tote containing just what they need!

Almost all of my free time for the next year or so was spent condensing and organizing my belongings from a forty-eight hundred square foot house to fit into a house one third the size. Bill repeatedly stood in amazement as I showed him how I could keep what I wanted and still make room for everything in his home.

We redecorated and bought some new furniture. New carpeting was laid, new liners and draperies were hung, all the woodwork was painted, each room was covered with wallpaper, pictures were hung, and the house finally began to look like me, whatever that is. Let's just say that Bill's grandchildren were so amazed that they just kept looking all around in total disbelief the first time they visited our newly decorated home and said, "Papa, there's color!"

Bill and I adjusted to each other quite easily. I don't think there is another person alive that is more like me than Bill. God truly blessed us. He loves my children, I love his children, and most important, our children love each other. He assisted me with our ministry and I began to learn about his favorite hobby, car racing. We did everything together and our home was a place of love and peace. I had waited all my life for this. I had been through so much heartache and I finally felt accepted, loved, wanted, comfortable, and content in my marriage.

Bill definitely was different than the men in my past relationships. Being married to a true man of God demonstrating all the fruits of the Spirit makes all the difference. I thought my heart was shattered beyond repair, but the Lord used my Godly husband to repair what I thought was hopelessly broken forever.

Walking had become very difficult. It was time to have my left knee replaced. I had been on crutches for so long and I couldn't put off the inevitable any longer. After a very painful operation, I spent the next six months recovering. Mornings were okay, afternoons were tolerable, but the evenings were pretty bad. Bill was with me during therapy sessions and saw to it that I faithfully did my exercises. His gentle and constant support led me down the road to recovery.

About one and one-half years later, I had to have my right knee replaced, the leg with the nerve damage. Again, it was difficult to walk and I couldn't put it off any longer. The doctor had some serious concerns about operating on the already injured leg, but was willing to do it and he took every precaution to prevent further damage to the nerves. I was on pins and needles, but had faith in God that He would guide my physician's hands and would protect me. The operation was done on a Thursday and went smoothly. Since the pain was minimal, I did well at therapy in the hospital. The night of the operation, I walked around the long hallway unassisted. The next day, I returned home and went to church that Sunday without a walker. Life was getting better.

The next Tuesday, I went to physical therapy with no incidence. Thursday was my next scheduled session. When the therapist pressed back on my knee, I heard a pop and felt a hot searing pain in my leg. "I think you just ripped all the inside stitches out of the muscle of my knee," I moaned. "No, that's impossible," he said. I limped out of the therapy center and I called for a visit to my knee surgeon. At my appointment, I told him what I thought had happened during my therapy visit and he immediately ordered an MRI the same day. When I returned a week later, I was told that the MRI verified my suspicions. The doctor explained, "The stitches on the inside across the top of your knee are no longer there. The muscle was torn apart like a piece of meat and cannot be repaired. The shredded edges are impossible to stitch and it is unlikely that it will ever heal. Your gait will be compromised. I can't tell how bad you will limp at this time. We will have to wait and see." I was fitted with a full leg brace to wear indefinitely and was given morphine for the pain in addition to the medicine I was already taking for the nerve damage in that same leg. Adjusting to the steel brace that supported my leg from my foot to mid-thigh was not easy. I wore it every waking minute. It was heavy and uncomfortable and hot in the warm weather, but I needed the support it gave me to walk. I tried to maintain a positive attitude, but what else could happen to me?

Several months later, as Bill and I were getting ready for bed, I felt suddenly ill. A feeling of weakness overcame me and the pain in my head was almost unbearable. I told Bill that I was going into our spare bedroom because I didn't foresee a restful night and I didn't want to keep him awake. I spiked a high fever and developed stomach problems. I vomited profusely thirteen times that night and had severe diarrhea. I didn't leave my bedroom for three long weeks. I can't ever remember being so sick, except in the hospital after the nerve damage. I couldn't eat. I sipped water only occasionally. I slept most of the time. Bill called the doctor and tried several kinds of medicine to help my stomach, but the pain continued. The doctor then prescribed medicine that they give chemotherapy patients for nausea, but that didn't help either. I refused to go to the hospital. It was too difficult and I just wanted to sleep. I didn't have the strength to get up and go. My kidneys shut down, and Bill later told me that he had never seen anyone so sick. He thought I was going to die. I never did get a diagnosis.

One of the nights that I was very ill, the Lord spoke to me as I lay in bed. He impressed on me to take note of the way my stomach hurt and how I felt. He wanted me to realize how sick the children in other countries become when they drink contaminated water, the only water they have to drink, water in which people bathe and animals wade and excrete. I had been watching James Robinson on "*Life Today*" almost every day for many months and had been emotionally moved seeing the poverty and the filthy water that the people drink. I was shaken by this realization and made a promise that I would give regularly to this cause. "Lord, is that why I experienced this sickness? I promise I will support this ministry. Thank you, Lord for allowing me to feel their pain. Help me to make a difference and to bring glory to your name," I prayed. These words came to my mind:

Dig a Well

Cheryl Marie

I see the river before me and I slowly look around
At the filth and the poverty,
At the children on the ground
Playing in a mudhole where germs and diseases lie
No wonder that death runs rampant
And daily people die

I see an animal carcass floating not too far away.
I see some women bathing
And doing laundry for the day.
The stench of excrement is strong
And my feet begin to sink.
That's when I see the children
Fill their cups and take a drink.

I wake up from my sleep
With an exasperating scream;
Oh please, Dear Lord, I pray, Dear Lord
That this was just a dream!
But as I rise, I realize that this awful dream is true;

Oh Lord, please speak to me right now
And tell me what I can do.

Dig a well, dig a well
Give cups of cold water in my name.
You have heard and seen the suffering,
The grief, and all the need.
Dig a well, dig a well for me

If you love the Father
Then His love should flow from you.
And when you see such suffering,
He'll tell you what to do.
Help in any way you can;
That's just what Christians do.
Bless all those around you-
That's what He's done for you.

I slowly regained my strength, but my stomach remained very irritated. Everything I ate made me extremely nauseous. At best, I nibbled on whatever I felt I could tolerate. I drank over the counter remedies to coat my stomach. I chewed antacids. I went on diets eliminating certain foods. Nothing helped. After two years of constant gnawing pain and nausea and on one occasion, passing blood, some tests were run and the doctors could find nothing except an extremely inflamed stomach. Not knowing what else to do, it was decided that my gall bladder was causing these symptoms. Against my better judgment, I had my gall bladder removed. When I went in to see the surgeon for my follow up visit, I asked how soon after surgery would I feel better. He said that my symptoms should have improved immediately. It was no surprise to me that I was still sick. The surgeon suggested that I taper off the morphine I was taking for the torn muscle. He felt that a combination of a bad case of the flu and the morphine I was taking for the ripped muscle in my knee could be the culprit.

Chapter 23

What is Wrong with Everyone?

"Honey, you are not making sense," my husband said to me with much concern in his voice. I looked at him with surprise and disbelief and repeated myself slowly, with emphasis on each word. I could tell by the look in his eyes that I communicated my thoughts no better the second time. I became discouraged and frustrated and decided to abruptly leave the room before I said something that I would regret. As I swung myself around and stomped away, I muttered under my breath, "What is wrong with him, Lord? I know what I said. Why is he saying I am not making sense? That just doesn't make sense! I know I have been very emotional lately, but hey, who wouldn't be? So much has happened in so short of a time. I know I have done a lot of crying for months, but I have had valid reasons to cry! I know I have been absent-minded, forgetting even important appointments, but I have too many things on my mind. I know I can't remember anything, but it's because I am protecting my brain from information overload! I have had trouble reading my Bible or any other magazine or book because I can't concentrate, but it's because I am so tired. I can't sleep and when I do, bad dreams and nightmares of my past fill my nights with restlessness. I know I haven't sung or played my piano for such a long time, but I just don't feel like it. I know I haven't even listened to the radio or my favorite CDs or watched any TV, but somehow, I don't want to hear any sounds at all. That is why I don't want to see my family or friends. I just want to be alone. I don't want to be around anyone or talk on the phone or go anywhere. I am a grown woman and I can do what I want and what I want is to be left alone. Why can't anyone understand that?"

Lord, I Want to Feel Your Presence There

Cheryl Marie

Lord, I'm angry, disappointed, in despair.

I'm even doubting, Lord, if you're really there.

I'm crushed, broken-hearted,

And you feel so far from me.

My prayer today-Your will, I pray

I want to see for me.

When my pain is all that I can feel,

I wonder if you, God, are really real

And questions without answers fill my mind

And I'm struggling-your hope I need to find.

When I try to sleep, all night I ask you why
I can't find rest and all I do is cry
I don't feel any better with the breaking light of day
Once was easy, oh, but now

I cannot find the words to pray
This valley is the deepest one I've known,
But I see through all the hard times that I've grown.
I want to feel your arms around me-this is my prayer.
Lord, I ask today, let me feel your loving care
And in this valley, let me feel your presence there.

Bill finally convinced me to see the doctor. I went just because he asked me so nicely and he did look worried. *He will see that there is nothing wrong with me; it's everyone else! Everybody expects me to be like I always was, but I have a lot on my plate right now!*

Chapter 24

The Dreaded Diagnosis

It took all I had in me to get myself dressed and presentable. Usually very particular about what I wear and how I look, I just threw on the first thing I saw hanging in my closet and forget the jewelry. I wasn't out to impress anyone; I just needed to prove to them that I was fine.

As we walked into the doctor's office, I began to tremble. Since I was still wearing the steel brace, I limped over to the window to report in to the receptionist. I found myself trying to hold back tears, my hands were sweating, and my lips were quivering. *I thought to myself, what is wrong with me?* Then I quickly reminded myself that there was nothing wrong with me, just everyone else! She asked me to take a seat and they would call me in shortly. Sitting in the chair next to Bill, I focused on the TV and didn't say a word. I didn't want him to see the emotional state I was in. I would just take a few minutes and settle myself down and I would be fine, in control as I had been known to be. *"Lord, just intervene here and allow me to receive a good report so Bill can know that I am fine,"* I silently prayed.

I had started seeing this doctor when we moved to the area twenty-six years ago. He knew my whole family quite well. He had also been Bill's doctor for many years. "Hi Cheryl, how are you?" said my doctor as he shook my hand. Tears began to gush like a broken dam. I had a hard time answering as I wiped my eyes, blew my nose, and apologized for my outburst. I explained that I have had a lot of heartache lately and I was very emotional, but Bill asked me to come because he thought that I wasn't making sense when I talked to him. I really hadn't said much at all to anyone over the past few weeks. *Don't you have to have more evidence than one incident when you are making such a bold statement about anyone?* I thought. I'd have to try to remember to ask my hus-band that later, after he hears that I am fine. Because I was still upset, Bill had to take over and explain to the doctor what he thought he had heard and observed.

The doctor turned to me and started to ask me all kinds of questions. Surprisingly, I pulled my thoughts together and had an answer for every question he asked.

"Yes, I was emotional and yes, I did cry constantly.

Anyone with a heart would cry with all the physical and emotional pain of their childhood and young adulthood stuffed deep down inside, not knowing how to be released.

Anyone with a heart would cry if they felt like they were being pulled in every direction and expected to be the an-swer to what everyone needs in their lives.

Anyone with a heart would cry if they were still feeling the failure of their attempts to save their twenty-two-year mar-riage.

Anyone with a heart would cry if they ignored the Holy Spirit's promptings and put themselves and their children in an abusive marriage.

Anyone with a heart would cry if they lived through seven and one-half years of intense stress and abuse.

Anyone with a heart would cry when they have been betrayed by those closest to them.

Anyone with a heart would cry if their father walked out of their life for no apparent reason and vowed to never talk to them again.

Anyone with a heart would cry if they have been through the stress, pain of four major surgeries in less than two years.

Anyone with a heart would cry if they endured the con-stant excruciating pain of permanently crushed nerves in their leg with no hope of relief.

Anyone with a heart would cry if the muscle in their leg was shredded and they would never be able to walk normally.

Anyone with a heart would cry if their successful ministry dissolved and was no more.

Anyone with a heart would cry if they lost their relationship with two of their children.

Anyone with a heart would cry with all the trauma exploding in their life at the present time.

Anyone with a heart would cry if they could trust no one.

Anyone with a heart would cry if they knew with absolute certainty that God was with them but could not feel Him.

Anyone with a heart would cry when their heart was broken so many times that they would rather die than to be hurt again.

Anyone with a heart would cry if their beloved grandmother passed and they were still carrying the guilt of failing to take care of her in her last days.

Anyone with a heart would cry if they had a huge hole in their heart because their precious "other mother" lost her long and hard battle with cancer.

Anyone with a heart would cry if they helplessly watched their child dying before their eyes,

Yes, I have trouble remembering things, but so does Bill! He writes everything on his calendar and that's the only reason he remembers! And yes, I have trouble concentrating and sleeping. The way I see it, I can't sleep because I have things on my mind and I can't concentrate because I am lacking sleep! That makes sense to me. I just don't feel like singing, playing the piano, listening to Christian music, watching TV, visiting, shopping, walking and talking! What's wrong with that?"

"The neurotransmitters in your brain are not connecting, Cheryl. What is happening is that you have had what they used to call a nervous breakdown. Now they call it clinical depression. You need both medication and therapy and we'll try to get you feeling better," my doctor explained.

I sat there stunned. Bill was right. I was wrong. I was thankful for him insisting that I see the doctor. I must be so out of it that I don't even know what's going on with my own mind and body! That was a scary thought to me. It made me sit up at attention and try to understand and concentrate on what the doctor was saying. I realized then that I was having trouble doing that. Bill took over, got directions for the medications, asked the right questions, and made arrangements to start therapy.

I succumbed to the reality of my diagnosis, and realized I needed help desperately. Life was hard and filled with so much pain, especially lately. It seemed as though every few days, something traumatic happened or I lost contact with someone very close to me. My heart had been crushed so many times. I felt completely helpless and confused. My days and nights were filled with grief, sorrow and sadness. Tears were uncontrollable at times. I felt like I was a spinning spiral that was being sucked downward into the abyss. Darkness and gloom engulfed me. I felt powerless to crawl out of the deep hole I was in. I tried and tried to ascend, but kept sliding back down into despair once again. After many attempts, I became very frustrated, drained, and hopeless. It was impossible, in my own strength, to overcome this wretchedness, despondency, and desolation I was experiencing. I knew God was with me, but I couldn't feel Him.

"When you pass through the waters, I will be with you; and when you pass through the rivers, they will not sweep over you. when you walk through the fire, you will not be burned; the flames will not set you ablaze. For I am the Lord, your God, the Holy One of Israel, your Savior." Isaiah 43;2-3 (NIV)

I thought about the Bible story of Joseph and how he must have felt. Betrayed by his own family, he was thrown into a deep pit and left to die. My pit was a mental dungeon and Joseph's was a physical hole in the ground. The shock, unbelief, anger, fear, rejection, dismay, astonishment, disappointment, and confusion Joseph must have felt, I knew so well. Therefore, I wrote:

Down in the Pit Like Joseph

Cheryl Marie

I was down in the pit like Joseph
In darkness and despair.
Pain inside my broken heart
Sent me way down deep somewhere,
Down in the pit like Joseph.

I was down in the pit like Joseph.
People who say they care
Put requirements and demands on me
That helped to put me there,
Down in the pit like Joseph.

God, what am I to learn down here
Where all I do is weep?
Please let me feel your love
And know your promises you'll keep.
The only place to look is up;
Let me see the light of day.
Help me trust in your time and plan;
You'll show me the way.

Down in the pit like Joseph,
There was nothing I could say.
Believing not the truth I told,
They closed their ears, they walked away.
I was down in the pit like Joseph.

My pit may not be a hole outside
Like Joseph was put in.
My pit, it is a hole inside
That my mind can't comprehend.
But like Joseph, I am trapped down there,
I feel helpless as can be.
Only God can pull me out;
His mercy He extends to me

I was down in the pit like Joseph
In the silence of the night.
God heard my cries, He felt my tears,
He let me know that I'd be alright
Down in the pit like Joseph.

He'll lift me out of the darkness.
He has blessings beyond what I can see.

And I can tell all those around me

What my Jesus, what He's done for me.

I was down in the pit like Joseph

In the silence of the night.

God heard my cries, He felt my tears,

He let me know that I'd be alright

Down in the pit like Joseph.

God is so amazing. He had His hand on Joseph. At the end of his rope, God was there for him. Circumstances fell into place under His direction and He used the worst thing that ever happened in Joseph's life for the greatest blessing in his life. *Could it be that God would do the same for me?* Now that was something to bring hope to my troubled soul!

Chapter 25

Understanding Cheryl

I told the doctor that I would agree to therapy as long as I could see a female therapist. So much of the pain that I had stuffed down deep inside, only a woman would understand. A lot of pain had been inflicted by men and I couldn't see myself relating to the gender that had hurt me so badly. I have been hurt by females also, but not as many times and not at the same magnitude.

I asked Bill to come to the therapist's office visit with me, fearful that I wouldn't be able to carry on a sensible conversation. She was nice, very pleasant, and warm. I immediately felt at ease. As well as I could communicate, I told her that I was a Christian and that I wouldn't listen to or do anything that was against my beliefs. To my surprise, she nodded and stated that she was a Christian, too. How good God is! We immediately connected and I trusted her. I had problems trusting anyone. I knew God had chosen this woman to help me.

I began to deal with all the buried pain I had experienced in my life, beginning in my childhood. That pain played a role in the decisions I made throughout the years. I never thought about what happened to me when I was younger would affect me my whole life! I began to plainly see the little girl with damaged emotions and understood why I blamed myself for choices that I made that had negative effects on me and my family's lives. I questioned why I struggled to do what I thought was best for everyone, but ended up causing them pain. I began to understand the reasons behind the choices I made, why I stress about certain situations, why I am a perfectionist, why I am very sensitive to people and pain, why I can't stand bad language, why I am a peacemaker, why I am a vault with someone's secrets, why I have fears, why I have security issues, why I value loyalty, why I have trouble trusting, why I care so much about my family and friends, why I am so very close to God, why I crave His love and peace. I began to understand myself for the first time in my life and realized that I did the best I could with the situations that I faced. My motives were pure and loving, just dysfunctional at times.

"He heals the brokenhearted and binds up their wounds."
Psalm 147:3 (NIV)

Understanding began to replace guilt. Forgiveness for myself began to replace condemnation. Peace began to replace chaos. Confidence began to replace apprehension. Patience began to replace anxiety. Acceptance began to replace sorrow. Belief began to replace disbelief. Trust began to replace fear. Tranquility began to replace turmoil. Letting go began to replace holding on. Hope replaced despair.

I began to release what I could not change, to walk away from toxic relationships, to concentrate on what I have instead of what I don't have, what I did instead of what I didn't do. I had forgiven all those who had hurt me, but had no idea what to do with all the pain. I felt like my whole body was stuffed with all the horrible heartache I had experienced in my whole life.

Where does all the pain go? Does it stay in the heart, the mind, the body? Does it dissipate? Even though the sting lessens as time goes on, the memories recreate the initial heart-wrenching stab of the infliction.

I hadn't been able to read my Bible or any other book for months because I could not comprehend the words. My mind felt like a boxed puzzle that had been shaken and dumped on a table. The pieces were all there, but they weren't in the proper place and I was unable to fit the pieces together.

Chapter 26

A New Song in My Heart

"Why, my soul, are you downcast? Why so disturbed within me? Put your hope in God, for I will yet praise Him, my Savior and my God." Psalm 42:5 (NIV)

Even though the neurotransmitters were out of sync and my brain could not produce rational thoughts, God began to speak to my spirit. I began to hear lyrics put to music in my head. These are the lyrics that I have inserted in this book. I asked Bill to bring me a notebook and a pen and I began to record the words that were given to me by the Spirit of God. The music was also embedded in my memory. Over the next three weeks, I received the words and music to seventeen songs. I was still in deep depression; I was still unable to even go to my piano and work on them; I was still unable to carry on a fluent conversation, but God chose to speak to me. He is so good and faithful. Those songs were like medicine poured into my spirit. Those songs expressed the agony I felt, but was unable to put into words. Those songs spoke life and hope to me. I knew as He imparted the lyrics and music to those songs, that I would get better and that those songs would help others that were hurting. I had a glimpse of what God was doing and why I was experiencing this fiery trial.

In time, I began to climb out of that dark, deep, lonely pit of clinical depression. I had been lying in bed or on the couch crying for many months, but now I could feel the presence of God. As the days passed, hope was restored. Slowly, I began to get my life back. I cried less and prayed more. I had strength and vigor to get back to doing my favorite things. After several months, I began to feel normal. I went to my piano to arrange and work on the songs that the Lord had given me. After I created the tracks and recorded the music, I sang those songs.

As I sang them over and over, my deepest emotions came forth. I thought there were no tears left after all the months I had lamented. All the horrendous pain I had stuffed all those years poured out of my being. Each song I tried to sing brought forth gut-wrenching, agonizing groans from the deepest canyons of my heart. I wept for anything, everything, and anyone that ever caused me pain. I sobbed until there were no tears left to shed as I sang the songs over and over for months.

God was healing me. He was cleaning out all the cavities of my body, mind, heart, and soul where I had stuffed every painful comment said to me, every mean deed done to me, all the demeaning treatment I had experienced, all the broken promises, all the emotional, verbal and mental abuse I survived all those years. I wept for my lost childhood and extremely sad and confusing teen years, my lonely child-bearing years, my tumultuous mid-life years. I mourned for failed relationships and lost years of happy family experiences. My old life and all its painful memories were being drained from me like you drain a bathtub of dirty water. I was now empty and ready for God to fill me up again with His refreshing living water.

Chapter 27

I Am A Miracle

I was in this state for months and it seemed like I had been in the deepest pit of darkness and despair forever. But now, God, in His mercy, was lifting me out.

I'm Too Anointed to Be Disappointed

Cheryl Marie

Satan's out to get me;

This is true without a doubt.

Bible says he's like a roaring lion

Wants to chew me up and spit me out.

But in Jesus I find refuge...I pray and I wait to see

When trouble tears my world apart

God puts a great big hedge round me.

He never promised sunshine;

Said that trials would come my way.

But He said He'd never leave me

And He's with me every day

When my heart is heavy

With worries and with care,

I give it all to Jesus; He answers when I pray.

I'm too anointed to be disappointed.

Too blessed to be stressed and too glad to be sad.

I've got Jesus who cares about me-

He says "Come to me and rest."

I just lean on my blessed Savior

And trust He knows what's best

Shortly after this cleansing experience, my heart was bursting with praise, thanking God for all that happened to me, the good and the bad. I learned that this praise was the key to unleashing God's favor, blessing, and healing.

I began to wean from the medication for the depression. I wanted to prove that God did a work in my life and no one could say that I was feeling better because of the prescriptions I was taking. Time would tell the truth and it did.

I felt like a totally different person. Overwhelming peace triumphed over my soul. Energy engulfed my being. A feeling of health and vitality flooded my body. Spiritual empowerment filled my heart. Victory replaced my defeated attitude.

I accepted the fact that the brace was a permanent accessory to my wardrobe. I even joked that if I had to wear it all the time, they could have at least given me a few of them in different shades so I could have color coordinated them with my outfits! I praised my Lord that I could still walk and that the decreasing doses of morphine were still keeping the pain at a tolerable level. I would not feel sorry for myself. There were a lot of other people that were a lot worse off than me. I thanked my Lord for my circumstance and I asked Him to teach me the lesson He would have me to learn through this trial.

I truly offered praise for everything and every situation. Peace and joy filled my soul.

"I waited patiently for the Lord; He turned to me and heard my cry. He lifted me out of the slimy pit, out of the mud and mire; He set my feet on a rock and gave me a firm place to stand. He put a new song in my mouth, a hymn of praise to our God. Many will see and fear and put their trust in Him." Psalm 40:1-3 (NIV)

As I meditated on this verse, I realized that God has specific instructions for us for deliverance from our problem. First, we must *"cry out in prayer"* to Him. Our cry is what grabs His attention. He *"hears that prayer and He turns to us."* Knowing that God hears us and has given us His attention, we then must *"wait patiently"* for

God's answer on His timetable. *"He lifted me out of the slimy pit, out of the mud and mire."* God does answer prayer and He lifts us out of the tumultuous and chaotic place in which we are stuck. *"He set my feet on a rock,"* a place of safety and strength in Him and blesses us with peace. Jesus will replace our desperate cry with a *"new song of praise"* that will bring glory to Him and cause others to *"trust in the Lord,"* to stand amazed at the power of the living God and desire the relationship that we have with Him.

My Lord is so wonderful! I cried out to Him and He heard me and gave me His attention! Thank you, Jesus! He literally lifted me out of the darkest, deepest, slimy pit of my life; out of the mud and mire! He set my feet on a Rock and gave me a firm place to stand! Jesus Christ is that rock on which I stand in faith. I would not slip back into that pit! His Spirit gave me new songs of praise to Him even when I couldn't think straight or carry on a meaningful conversation! I know He gave me those songs for a reason. He gave me a powerful testimony of His mercy and His healing power and I know in my heart that He has called me to share what He has done for me! His promise is that many will hear and will trust their lives to Jesus Christ! Glory to His name!

This promise in His Word is powerful and brings so much hope, yet it is so humbling to me. To think that God could use my testimony to bring hope, healing and salvation to others makes me want to fall to my knees and worship Him and thank Him for all I have been through and to praise Him for His healing touch. My prayer is that others will come to Him and trust Him to do the same for them.

Chapter 28

Pain in My Past: Peace in My Present

"Therefore, if anyone is in Christ, a new creation has come; the old has gone, the new is here!" 2 Corinthians 5:17 (NIV)

The day I accepted Jesus Christ as my Lord, I became a new person on the inside. No longer did I live for myself, but for Christ. God never said that we would not have troubles in our lives, but promised that He would always be with us. When I think back to who I was forty-eight years ago, and to who I am now, it is like I was someone else. I believe that everything that has happened to me has shaped me into a totally and completely different person that loves God more, trusts God more, seeks God more, prays to God more, and studies God's Word more. I act differently, speak differently, and think differently. I have different motives and different goals. Things that used to be important are not anymore. Other matters have become imperative. I have more boldness, more urgency to share the Lord with others, more discernment, more wisdom, more power, and more peace. These rewards and blessings have come not through those mountaintop experiences when everything is going well, but through those gloomy and lonely valleys.

"And the God of all grace, who called you to His eternal glory in Christ, after you have suffered a little while, will himself restore you and make you strong, firm and steadfast." 1 Peter 5:10 (NIV)

Dark places and the hard trials in our lives is where God grows us, teaches us, draws us close to Him, and purifies us. In those valleys, God develops us to have more strength in our faith.

"Not only so, but we also glory in our sufferings because we know that suffering produces perseverance, perseverance, character, and character, hope." Romans 5:3,4 (NIV)

It is there, in the midst of fiery trials, that some may feel that God has deserted them, but He is present and walks with us.

"Who shall separate us from the love of Christ? Shall trouble or hardship or persecution or famine or nakedness, danger or sword? As it is written: For your sake we face death all day long; we are considered as sheep to be slaughtered. No, in all these things we are more than conquerors through Him who loved us. For I am convinced that neither death nor life, neither angels nor demons, neither the present or the future, nor any other power,

neither height nor depth, nor anything else in all creation, will be able to separate us from the love of God that is in Christ Jesus our Lord." Romans 8:35-39 (NIV)

I truly thank my Lord for the good times and the bad, when I was happy and when I was sad. After learning many truths, I have denounced the lies of Satan and continue to look for the good in seemingly bad circumstances. He is God and He never changes and He has me in His hands. I can rest, without worry, and trust Him completely. My prayer is that God will continue to allow me to trade beauty for ashes, gladness for mourning, and praise for despair. I have made it a priority to replace the pain in my past with praise for my Lord, who has brought me out of darkness and into His light.

The darkness: Pain in my past- My life has not been easy. I grew up in a dysfunctional home, the oldest of four girls. My parents were both good people, but very toxic for each other. Because of the stress created in this tense, hateful, unhealthy, antagonistic atmosphere of our home, I suffered severe emotional, verbal, and physical abuse. Children internalize what parents say about them and how the parent's make them feel. I have many, many invisible wounds. This greatly affected every aspect of my life. I was put in the position and forced to assume responsibility for not only what happened in my home, but also for what did not happen.

His light: Peace in my present-I realize now that I was not responsible for the atmosphere of my home. I was a child and keeping peace was not my job. To suffer all types of abuse because of the anger, frustrations, and disappointments of my parents was unfortunate, undeserving, and should have never happened. After I realized the effect that my childhood had on me, I have made every effort to have a better future.

The darkness: Pain in my past-When I was a child, I had to repeatedly apologize to my father for my "terrible" be-havior before he would talk to me again. I became aware that he was upset with me when he coldly ignored me. I bit my nails until they bled, trembled uncontrollably, my stomach would get sick and my little heart would beat faster and faster as I tried to figure out why he was displeased with me. To this day, I don't know what I ever did to deserve such estrangement, but I had to beg for forgiveness to make amends. I experienced this treatment over and over throughout my life, never knowing what my offense was.

Dad has done some awful, dreadful things to our family as well as our extended family and it appears everyone disregards, denies, or accepts the behavior because "that's the way Dad is." Ignoring his behavior, making excuses for him, catering to him, and apologizing when you are innocent has allowed his conduct to escalate.

After my clinical breakdown, my counselor called my father and tried to set up a meeting in his town with myself and my three sisters. She felt it would be best to have an overseer with experience in family therapy. He adamantly refused and told her he wasn't interested in restoring any relationship with us. He "was done with all of us for life." When she asked him, specifically, what I had done to him, he said, "She knows what she did." She hung up the phone, shaking her head, and told me that I have done everything that I could possibly do. My father was a "silent tyrant" and a "master manipulator." I then asked my pastor, "Will I be held accountable for the severed relationship?"

His light: Peace in my present- I realize that my father has a very serious problem. Over the years, he has done this same thing to many family members. Right now, he is not speaking to most of his brothers and sisters and none of his nine grandchildren or sixteen great grandchildren. He speaks Dee and Rose when he needs something from them, but not to Marsha and myself. What could have we all done to deserve this rejection and elimination from his life?

After all the pain, in spite of all the issues, I feel so sorry for Dad and I do love him. I used to disguise my writing on the outside of the envelope and send him notes every several months telling him I love him and that I am praying for him. That is until I started to find them back in my mailbox, unopened, with "REFUSED" written in bold lettering. I wish I knew what happened during his lifetime to cause him to act the way he does. I pray that God will heal his pain. I forgave him and put him in the Lord's hands. I still feel badly at times, but I have resolved that I may never see him alive again.

How will I feel when he's gone? I really don't know because it feels like he died already. He is ninety-four and at the end of his life and I pray that he will accept God's love and forgiveness and be reunited with his family before it is too late.

One day as I was meditating and asking God to heal my pain, He spoke to my heart as He showed me a vision of my father. Dad was sitting on a hard, straight-backed wooden chair in the middle of a large cemented area. Surrounding him was a red brick wall that was probably about eight feet tall. I could see that people had tried to chisel at a few bricks here and there. There was mortar and chipped pieces on the ground outside the wall, but no one seemed to be successful in even carving a hole big enough to see Dad inside sitting on the chair. They couldn't see that there was a heavy massive chain that was wrapped around his torso several times. They failed to see the heavy padlock that hung from the left side of the chair. Black birds pecked relentlessly day and night on the top of his head, but not a sound did my father make. I knew that God was showing me that the enemy had my dad bound in chains and was putting torturous thoughts in his head. My father didn't realize this was happening. The wall represents how he has shut everyone out of his life. People have made attempts to get close to him, but are not successful. I was moved with sadness. The Lord said to me,

"Cheryl, your earthly father loves you in the only way that he knows how to love. You must believe this or anger will well up inside of you for the pain that he has brought into your life and your entire family's lives. Pain in his life, emotional trauma, and illness that you are unaware of has made him who he is. It may not be right, but without me to change his heart and heal his emotions and mindset, his way of living and his behavior will not change. He has denounced me and has rejected my love. He has refused the urging of my Holy Spirit. He has cast away everyone that I have sent into his life to show him my love. He is lonely and so sad. I know your heart feels this. I know how it hurts you, but there is really nothing you can do to change his heart except to pray; This work is done by my Spirit alone. You must look to me as your Father, for my love is pure, unconditional, and never changing. All I require is for you to accept my love and love me back, pure and unconditional. Blessings come to you because of my love for you, not because of conditions you meet to earn it. My love is different than your father's love. Look

to me and I will fill that void, that hole that your father has left unattended. I will be your father and I will never leave you or forsake you. You can come to me anytime and I will be there for you. I know you miss how your dad used to take care of you and the security you felt that you didn't have to worry about every-thing. You knew he would fix what he could and make sure you and your children were taken care of. I will do much more for you if you would have that sense of depending on me. I love you so much more and can offer you so much more.

Search your heart, Cheryl. Do you really forgive him? Can you blot out from your memory all the pain that he has caused so many people that you love? I will help you, Cheryl, as you give me all that pain. He has done some horrible things, hurtful things, unthinkable things. Let me carry and lift that load from your shoulders. Just as you have done wrong and have been forgiven, you must forgive your father. I will help you. I will heal your broken heart. If you would want to write him one last time, you may, but let me guide and direct your words. Let no accusations, self-pride, pity, or anger be read between the lines. Offer forgiveness and ask for forgiveness. Clear the air so that you may have rest when his life is over. You can only do what you can to release yourself from any accusations and lies from the enemy. Your dad is responsible for his own soul. Release him and fret no more about the outcome. I want peace for you, my child, for you can only do so much; The rest is in my hands. Trust me, Cheryl, and I will take care of you for I am the father you never had, but always wanted. You can trust me with your children, your grandchildren, your husband, your family, your life and everything and everyone in it. I want only what is best for you and every good gift comes from me."

The darkness: Pain in my past-At thirteen years of age, I witnessed Dee being struck by a car. I felt guilty that I wasn't watching her at the time it happened and I spent the whole summer by her bedside as she recovered from very serious injuries. For many years after the accident, I couldn't get the sound of the tires screeching out of my head. I couldn't block out the snapshot of the back end of the car lifted by the applied pressure of the brakes and the sight of all the blood on the street coming from my four-year old sister.

His light: Peace in my present-Dee was not in my care when she was hit. I was thirteen and on my way to my friend's house. I just happened to be in the same block when I heard the tires skid and the sound of the blunt thud as she was struck. Because I saw the accident did not make me responsible. Thank the Lord, she lived and recovered well.

The darkness: Pain in my past-When I was in high school, our home was destroyed by fire. It was a very traumatic period of my life, not only because of the fire, but because of incidences that happened as a result of the fire. We lost our dog, our home and almost everything in it. I remember standing in the snow in bare feet, with no emotion, watching the flames shoot out of the windows of our home. It was like a bad dream. As I became aware of reality and the seriousness of the situation, I knew that it would be up to me to get my family through this. I was seventeen. During my junior and senior year of high school, I was distracted with the uncertainties of my home life. I missed out on the years of fun and social development needed by every teenager. College was out of the question. How could I even give a thought to my future when my present life was so unstable and we needed all the finances we had to recover from the loss from the fire.

His light: Peace in my present- It was about thirty years after the fire. My children and I were sitting in the family room of my Victorian home when we heard sirens and firetrucks passing the window. They jumped up, ran outside, and discovered that a house one block away was on fire. I stood on the sidewalk by my side door, watching the scene and saying a prayer for the family. Suddenly, my mind was taken back to the fire at my house. Standing as a young teen watching my house burn, I relived the smells, the sounds, the feelings of sadness, helplessness, and panic as I watched the flames whipping out the windows. The emotions that I had squelched when I was a teen welled up inside of me and burst forth. I sobbed for my family's loss. I cried for the death of our dog and the loss of our belongings. I wept for the weight of the task of getting my family through this terrible ordeal.

I do know now that trying to hold my family together during this time was a heavy misplaced burden on me. I know now that I carried a lot of responsibility and experienced a lot of worry that should not have been mine. I understand why I am prone to step up and take care of everything and why I am able to ignore my emotions and handle the situation before me. I have made every effort to make the best of my life in spite of all the obstacles I have encountered and the opportunities I missed.

The darkness: Pain in my past-I never truly grieved the miscarriages of my three babies. I didn't know how to mourn. I always suppressed all my feelings. For decades, as thoughts of my deceased children flooded my mind, I would either withdraw and cry or I would try to bury my grief and try to forget I ever experienced their loss.

His light: Peace in my present-I anticipate the reunion with my children. I feel complete peace knowing they are with Jesus, the lover of children. I don't cry over them, nor do I ignore their absence. Peace floods my soul.

The darkness: Pain in my past-When I learned that my seven-month old son, Scott, was diagnosed with a terminal disease, the shock rattled my faith. Only three years before, I had decided to serve Jesus Christ. I was enjoying my newfound relationship with the Lord. I wondered why God was allowing this. Didn't he love me? Wasn't He in the healing business also? What did I do wrong that my child is so sick? What happens to my relationship with the Lord if Scott doesn't survive? I did learn quickly that either I was going to release my faith one hundred percent and trust God to heal Scott or I was going to sit back and watch my baby boy die.

His light: Peace in my present- Our family prayed and made a conscious decision to trust and we knew that without God on our side, Scott had little hope of becoming a man. I believed God and He healed my son. At an old-time tent meeting in our town eleven years later, Scott was also miraculously healed once more of severe allergies and debilitating asthma for which he had been treated since he was a toddler. The faithfulness of God overwhelms me!

The darkness: Pain in my past-The termination of my marriage of twenty-two years left me disappointed, disillusioned, untrusting, and hurt. I had buried so much pain and heartache and I didn't know what to do with it. I didn't want the divorce. I just wanted a good marriage. I had forgiven and moved on, but still carried anger because the truth had never been disclosed of what really happened so that my hurting children could see why the marriage ended. I didn't want to disrespect their father to them, but I longed for them to know that I made the only possible decision.

His light: Peace in my present-I've come to understand that as long as God knows what really happened and I know the truth, it's okay. My children and I, on different occasions, have had opportunities to discuss snippets of the marriage. Now I prefer to not even do that. God has given me peace and I don't want the price of that peace to be the degradation of someone's character. CJ possessed many wonderful qualities. He was a great person, but lacked the traits needed for a good relationship. With the brokenness I brought from my past, I also failed miserably. I tried to write about the marriage from my feelings so that you as the reader could comprehend where I was and why one disappointment led to another. It's not important who was right or wrong. We are all imperfect creatures and we all need Jesus Christ's righteousness.

The darkness: Pain in my past-The loss of relationship with my two sons broke my heart and I blamed myself. Was I a bad mother? As they were growing up, was I wrong to step up to the plate and enforce the rules? What was I to do when I was their only disciplinarian and after their fair and just punishment, my boys were told that I was too hard on them? How could I as a mother fill the leadership role of a father? What was I to do when CJ used all my children as a sounding board for our relationship problems? Untruths and misconceptions conveyed about me had broken my heart. For years I masked the pain and cried when alone. I was unable to create unity and support between CJ and me and this caused extreme frustration and hopelessness. Not only did I lose my marriage, I lost one of my sons at that time and the other one during my marriage to Dan. Sorrow and grief filled my heart, I worried about their well-being, and I felt hopeless to go on without them being a part of my life.

This song was written during the time of my clinical depression; during the span that I was unable to communicate my thoughts or express myself.

Please Come Home to Me

Cheryl Marie

I think of all the days spent as a family;
Oh, the memories seem like yesterday.
The hugs and the kisses and the I love yous;
I miss them so much since you've been away.

The laughter and the smiles, the tears and the pain
It seems all families must go through.
They should have brought us closer and not apart;
My heart is broken since I don't have you.

I don't care where you've been;
I don't care where you are.
I need you so much, can't you see?

The cry of my heart is for you
To be a part of my life again.
Please come back to me.

So please don't hate me for I love you so.
I cry each day; it tears me apart.
I pray to God to bring you back to me,
Put everything behind us, have a brand-new start.

A mother's love, sent from God above,
It never, never ends.
No matter who you are, no matter what you've done,
On my love you can depend.
It never dies and that's the reason why
I can't rest and I can't let you go.
I'll be waiting patiently for the day
You come back to me
And we can be a family again.

His light: Peace in my present- I pray for my boys every day. I miss them terribly, but I have done all I know to do to mend the relationships. I certainly have made my share of "motherhood" mistakes and I pray that I have learned from them so that I am a better grandparent. How I would love the opportunity to talk to them, to know their hearts, to see beyond the choices they have made, to connect with them in love, and to hear, understand, apologize and ask forgiveness for anything I have unknowingly done to cause them pain. Until then, I stand on His promises and believe that Jesus will bring them back to me. I am at peace for I have given them to the Lord and I trust Him with my sons.

The darkness: Pain in my past-Living with the constant pain and fatigue of fibromyalgia takes its toll mentally as well as physically. It is a disease that allows one to look like they are a picture of health as they suffer with pain all over their body twenty-four hours a day. The person appears to be a hypochondriac, but is truly in misery. Most people that have the disease suffer with depression. Pain, lack of sleep and energy makes life extremely difficult.

His light: Peace in my present-I described the fibro-myalgia as a thorn in my flesh, my cross to bear. I accepted the symptoms and tried to have a good mental attitude. Because I was not terminal and I could still function after the thirty months in bed, I was appreciative and thankful to the Lord. There were a lot of people a lot worse off than me!

In the book of Job, we see how he lived a life pleasing to God. He had a strong foundation of faith. He was blessed with family, friends, possessions, and prestige. All of a sudden, Job was tested in every way. Satan was allowed to destroy his family and all his possessions, but Job trusted God. Then he suffered physically. His wife told him to curse God and die, but Job still trusted God. His friends were at first, sympathetic, but after a while, began to try to convince Job that all this tragedy was because he had sinned.

Another man told Job that he had become proud and that caused all the calamity. All were wrong!

I, like Job, was told by well-meaning friends that I should not "accept" fibromyalgia. I was told that I had to have sin in my life that was causing it. After agonizing in prayer and begging God to forgive me of sin that I "may" have undetected in my life, I was still sick.

As I studied the book of Job, I realized that suffering is not always a result of sin. We may never know, while we are here on earth, why God has allowed hard times in our life. His ways are beyond our comprehension. The Lord simply tells us to remain faithful and trust Him in the storm.

I began to pull away from those who added to my pain by making me feel guilty that some hidden sin was causing fibromyalgia. I didn't need friends who knocked me down when I was already there! We must be careful what we say to our fellow Christians for we will have to answer to the Lord for every word.

The darkness: Pain in my past-The mental, emotional, and physical abuse my children and I experienced for seven and one-half years was one of the worst times of our lives. Guilt, shame, and confusion filled my life. I asked myself why I married him when I knew in my heart that I was ignoring the Holy Spirit's warning signals. I dwelled on my mistake. I allowed Satan to condemn me and torment me to tears.

His light: Peace in my present-I had been in extreme emotional pain for many years. I was feeling so empty and alone. My self-esteem was ruined. I was vulnerable and starving for attention and communication that I never had. I was wanting a happy family more than anything. These reasons are not an excuse for my decision, but rather an understanding of why I did what I did. Although I endured much, this nightmare was the catapult that led me to fully surrendering every area of my being to the Lord Jesus Christ. Never again would I make a decision without the approval of the Holy Spirit. Never again would I ignore what the Lord was showing me. Never again would "I" be in control of my life.

"The Lord is my rock, my fortress and my deliverer; my God is my rock, in whom I take refuge. He is my shield and the horn of my salvation, my stronghold." Psalm 18:2 (NIV)

I have now truly experienced the truth of this passage of scripture.

Jesus is my rock, a strong, unmovable protector; He is my fortress, my place of safety where I run; He is my shield, coming between me and all harm that may occur; He is my horn of salvation, mighty and powerful; He is my stronghold, sitting high above my enemies.

I am closer to Jesus than I ever was before and I truly thank Him. As I was journaling my thoughts to the Lord one day, I asked him a question. I said "Lord, how do you see me and what would you like to say to me?"

God spoke to my heart as I wrote His response.

"You are so beautiful, my child, because my beauty shines through you. You are what I had in mind when I created you. The times you've failed and the times you've made wrong choices, I have still loved you. There were times it hurt me so to see you suffer the consequences of following your own will instead of mine, but you have learned the lessons I have taught you so far because you are a woman who seeks after my heart. That is pleasing to me. I see you as my treasured child, no one else quite like you. I have made you unique. I see you with spiritual eyes, not as the world sees you. The way I see you is what really matters. I see you with eyes of love that you could never fathom, a love that is unconditional, higher and vaster than the heavens I created. That is my love for you, my child. I see you as my hands and feet to bring hope and healing, not only to my children, but to those who do not know me as you do. I see you as my messenger, one who can tell of the miracles I can do, because you, yourself, are a miracle. Tell them, oh urge them to come and receive as you have."

God can do for you what He has done for me. He loves you just as much! Ask Him to be Lord of your life, to touch you, to heal you, to make Himself real to you.

The darkness: Pain in my past-The death of my grandmother was a monumental loss to me. I was the oldest grandchild and we were exceptionally close. The pain was compounded by my inability to change my circumstances. At the time, I was nearing the end of the abusive marriage, the atmosphere was extremely tense, and I wasn't able to move her to my home and take care of her for the last few weeks of her life. When I would visit her, she would beg to go with me and that not only broke my heart, but angered me that I lived in such turmoil and I couldn't fulfill her last request. Watching her wave good-bye to me, with longing tears in her eyes, crushed me. I loved her so much and cried, with regret, that I couldn't take care of her when she needed me most. I sang and spoke at my dear grandmother's funeral without a tear. I buried all the agony deep down inside and I never grieved for her.

His light: Peace in my present- I sometimes wonder where I would be if the Lord hadn't been with me that day. I can't change what happened. I wanted to do all I could for my grandmother and I realize now that under the circumstances I was in, I did do all I could. I visited her often, brought her the treats she loved the most, cleaned her house when I came, listened to the thoughts on her heart, called her most days, took care of any problem she voiced to me, and let her know how special she was. I have to look back with sweet thoughts of her. Her gentleness and kindness to me will always be a precious memory. The way she made me feel so important and loved will always be close to my heart. Her spunk, unforgettable! With gratitude for the Lord's faithfulness, I remember the day a few months before she died, that she prayed with me and asked Jesus to forgive her sins and save her soul. I know she is in Heaven and will greet me when I get there. I can't wait to feel her arms around me again.

The darkness: Pain in my past-The day my grandmother was buried was an awful day in my son's life also. A phone call at the funeral services put me in shock and distress. I had no knowledge that Brock had suffered as a victim for nine of his fifteen-year life and guilt and grief that only a mother would understand weighed heavily on me. My eyes were opened. *That explained his behavior! Yes, he had done some things I am not proud of at all, but now I see* *the picture. He needed professional help. He was hurting terribly. If only I had known! Why didn't I see it? How could this have happened?*

Dan was heartless and insensitive to my loss and pain and battered me verbally with remarks about my son until I thought I couldn't take much more. I hated him for being so cruel! *How much agony can one bear?*

His light: Peace in my present-I can't change what happened. I can only deal with the grief, guilt and responsibility I felt. The burden I carried was heavy, much too heavy to bear alone. I had to go to the Word of God for answers and apply his promise to my life in order to have any kind of healing and peace.

"I lift up my eyes to the mountains-where does my help come from? My help comes from the Lord, the Maker of heaven and earth." Psalm 121:1-2 (NIV)

"I have told you these things, so that in me you may have peace. In this world you will have trouble. But take heart! I have overcome the world." John 16:33 (NIV)

"Cast your cares on the Lord and he will sustain you. He will never let the righteous be shaken." Psalm 55:22 (NIV)

Applying these scriptures to my broken heart was a process for me over a long period of time. The lessons learned changed my life. No longer did I have to carry the weight on my own. Jesus took my years of tears and sorrow, the entire weight of my heavy burden when I learned to give it to him completely. Many times, I unconsciously took it back and, repeating old habits of taking full responsibility for everything, I lost my peace immediately. It was too much for me to handle on my own. Finally, I yielded, abandoned my hold on all the distress and completely laid Brock at Jesus' feet. I dare not take that burden back. The serenity, comfort, joy, and rest I feel has proven that God is faithful and He has healing for a broken heart. Thank you, Lord.

The darkness: Pain in my past-The cancer diagnosis, the years of unbearable suffering, and finally the death of one of my dearest friends left me feeling very distraught. She was more than my friend. Betty was like a mother to me-a confidant, someone I trusted with my most personal thoughts, someone who accepted me for who I am, someone who always had time to listen, who understood and supported me, someone who I loved deeply. Spontaneous tears of sadness burst forth during the following grief-filled months. Oh, how I missed her smile, the loving way she spoke to me, the encouragement she gave to me over the forty-one years I was privileged to know her, the unwavering belief she had in me, her hugs, her love.

His light: Peace in my present-Do I still miss her? Immensely! I am so thankful for the gift of her wonderful friendship. Before she died, she prayed and accepted the forgiveness of Jesus Christ. I will see her again and I look forward to that day. During her extended illness, I had the chance to write her a few letters telling her how much she meant to me. This has brought me peace.

The darkness: Pain in my past- Betrayal by a good friend caused a searing pain, like a knife stabbing into my back. Her gossip, insensitivity to my feelings and privacy, and then her flippant brushing off of her offensive behavior caused me to struggle to restore my trust and intimacy with this friend. The deep pain led me to question my trust in some of the other relationships I had and left me feeling guarded around people. I withdrew from everyone to protect my heart. The impact was compounded, happening the same time as the loss of my father and my two sons, the critical condition of my child, the terrible physical pain, and my slide into the pit of depression. I penned this song:

Keep Your Eyes on Jesus

Cheryl Marie

Sometimes I look at people

And circumstances that come about.

I feel so trapped and misunderstood;

I cry, God, please take me out.

No one understands me and I'm hurt, torn up inside,

But I forget that Jesus is with me

And for times like these He died.

So, when I feel so down-hearted

About things that happen in this place;

Although I'm accused so wrongly,

He understands and through His grace,

I look at those who hurt me
And through Jesus I forgive
And remember that it's not for others,
But for Jesus I must live.

I cry, God have mercy; I can't be hurt no more.
I'm crushed by those who are so close;
I can't go on no more, I'm sure.
But I hear the Lord so softly,
"There's a lesson I want you to learn;
Don't seek approval from the brethren,
But for mine, your heart must yearn."

Through many disappointments
And through tears of hurt inside,
I've learned to find any comfort and rest,
In Jesus, I must abide.
It's not enough to love Him;
For this world's a cruel place.
You must keep your eyes toward Heaven
On His tender and loving face.

For He says, "Keep your eyes

On the tower of strength that I give.

Don't give in to your hurt and anger, just forgive.

For don't you know that I'm the only one

Who knows all you go through?

And I allow it for it makes

A better Christian out of you.

For don't forget that I'm the only one

Who knows all you go through?

And I allow it for it makes

A better Christian out of you."

His light: Peace in my present- The most important relationships in my life, my father and mother, taught me the people I love will hurt me and therefore I have a great fear with close relationships. I don't trust easily. This betrayal was exceptionally painful to me. Forgiveness was offered to me through Jesus Christ, who faced the ultimate betrayal. Jesus forgave and I am commanded to forgive also. After much counseling, I learned that forgiveness is required, but restoring that kind of relationship is not. Forgiveness is freeing and time heals.

I am sensitive to the Lord's leading in choosing my friends. I may not have many, but I can trust the few I have. I have boundaries. I am now more careful about what I share and with whom. All my intimate thoughts and feelings are shared with Jesus who never will betray us for He is love.

Wisdom is a valuable tool. It is a gift from God that will save us much heartache. How my intuitive discretion has been sharpened! How aware I have become of manipulation! How careful I am to protect myself from control by others. How keen my sense of hypocrisy! How fast I identify a heart that truly cares as compared to a heart that thrives on gossip.

I am now able to identify with those who have lost trust in someone because of some kind of betrayal. I can relate from first-hand experience, counsel them, and assure them that there is a peace that they can have through forgiveness.

The darkness: Pain in my past-The nerve damage resulting from the arthroscopic surgery on my right knee was the most agonizing and horrific pain that anyone could imagine. I had to take several strong narcotic medications up to four times a day plus wear a pain patch to control the throbbing in my right leg. The pain never ceased. The medicine could only make it barely tolerable. I harbored much anger, not only because it happened and the agony I endured, but also because of the way I was treated in the hospital and at the doctor visit. I was fearful that the pain would become uncontrollable again. I worried that I would have to keep increasing the medication over time to manage the severity. Having to look ahead to a future with this nerve pain ever present was a tough sentence to deal with.

His light: Peace in my present- I began to thank my Lord for my circumstance and asked Him to teach me the lesson He would have me to learn through this horrific experience. *If I never had this experience, could I identify with those who are in excruciating pain? Would I be able to say that I know God can bring them through?*

Could I honestly say that I know how it feels? Would I be able to show true empathy?

"Rejoice always, pray continually, give thanks in all circumstances, for this is God's will for you in Christ Jesus." I Thessalonians 5:16-18 (NIV)

I was a Chaplain Assistant at our local hospital and I used my painful experience to bring hope to the patients I visited. With complete assurance, I was able to testify that God will be with them no matter what the circumstance and they will come through victoriously.

When I was sick with a very irritated stomach. I couldn't keep anything down and could not take my medication for a few weeks. When I began to feel better, I realized that the nerve in my leg had not been hurting.

God had once again healed me! The femoral and obturator nerves in my leg that were hopelessly and permanently crushed were no longer causing me constant pain! His blessings are amazing, his mercy is unending, and His grace is sufficient for every need! Hallelujah!

The darkness: Pain in my past-Recovering from a knee replacement definitely gives you time to think and to put life in perspective. The pain of the first knee operation had me down for almost six months. When the therapist ripped all the inside stitches out of my newest knee replacement, the diagnosis of the muscle tear never healing was the last thing I needed to hear. I had been through too much already.

His light: Peace in my present-Having two replacements has made me grateful that I can walk freely and go places without assistance. I don't know why God allowed the muscle to be torn so badly, but I believe He was with me and had a purpose.

"And we know that in all things God works for the good of those who love him who have been called according to His purpose." Romans 8:28 (NIV)

If my good was walking with a brace or a limp for the rest of my life, I could accept that for I had learned to trust my Lord.

I thank God for His mercy and His healing. I was elated to take off that brace and walk freely. People had seen me either on crutches, in a brace, or wheelchair for over three years and now they could not question that God had done a miracle and all the praise and glory would go to Him!

The darkness: Pain in my past-A mother would do anything to save the life of her child. To helplessly watch her own flesh and blood dying while all efforts to help that child failed, is the worst pain for a mother to experience. I have had to do just that for many years. There was no peace, only turmoil. There were no answers, only uncertainty. There was no rest, only worry. There was no happy, only sad.

His light: Peace in my present-One of the hardest lessons I have ever had to learn is to put each of my children totally into the hands of God and then to let go completely. I always said I trusted God with my children because He loved them more than I did, but I realized that I truly wasn't practicing what I preached. Facing my child's possible death over and over, I didn't have anywhere to look but to Him and He was there. I know I can completely give Him my children and rest in peace, for He is able to take care of them better than I ever could.

A common thread through all pain is that you feel so alone and that no one cares or understands. I know I felt that way. I longed for love, understanding, and empathy, but who can fill your being with all those things? No one on this earth can be all that one needs in time of sickness, sorrow and despair! Only Jesus can supply all our needs! The Lord spoke softly to me in my time of need. He said,

"Rest in me, my child. Come into my arms, take a deep breath, and rest. I long to hold you, to embrace you. Come lay your head on my chest. Feel my heartbeat. May the rhythm cause you to relax and rest a while. I am here always. My arms are open wide always for you are my child. Let my love embrace you. Can you feel it? Love, not as the world gives, love not tainted, but pure love from Almighty God, your Father. A love that allowed His Son to come to shed His blood for you. A love that speaks, a love that demonstrates, a love that is enduring and unending, a love that sees the best in you, a love that will never die. Come and rest in that love and let it bring peace to your troubled soul."

Do you need the Lord's embrace right now? His arms are open wide. Come and rest and lay your head on his chest. Feel His heartbeat, experience His peace and love.

Chapter 29

Lessons Learned in the Fire

If I knew then what I know now, I would have strived to know Jesus Christ intimately from the moment I met Him. I would have prayed more, spent additional time basking in His presence, and purposely arranged many more intimate moments to listen intently and hear His still small voice.

If I knew then what I know now, I would have learned as much about Jesus as I possibly could and I would have done it more quickly and intently with an urgency so that I would have been a stronger Christian for more of my life. Doing so would have resulted in much more knowledge, and would have enabled me with the guidance of the Holy Spirit, to influence more people with my testimony.

If I knew then what I know now, I would have memorized many more scriptures so that I would have had more of God's Word and wisdom deep inside my being.

If I knew then what I know now, I would have made serving God my number one priority. I always thought He was first place in my life, but now I realize that was not the case.

If I knew then what I know now, I would have made different choices, ones based on more prayer instead of my own reasoning.

If I knew then what I know now, I would have strived to be more educated to fulfill God's calling.

If I knew then what I know now, I would have been bolder to share my relationship with the Lord in more situations. Who knows how many more people would have heard about His gift of forgiveness and trusted Jesus as their Savior and made Him Lord of their lives!

If I knew then what I know now, I would have not taken any credit for any of my accomplishments. It is only through Him that I have been able to do anything. It is only through His power that I can even begin to share my story in this book.

If I knew then what I know now, I would have taken full advantage of the one chance to live my life totally and completely for the glory of God. On the other hand, I am so thankful that when we mess up and fall on our face, God is always there to pick us up, brush us off, and give us another chance to do what is pleasing in His sight. I have finally discovered that instead of defining myself by the wrong choices I've made, I have to look at the way I have learned from those mistakes.

If I knew then what I know now, I would have chosen to obey the voice of God. Whatever the circumstances may be, He always sees the whole picture and knows what is best for us. There is no place comparable to walking with the King. There is no road so sweet. There is no other peace. There is no other way. I have learned it is wonderful to serve Him.

I Will Serve Thee

Cheryl Marie

I want to thank you, it's overdue,

For all the trials you have brought me through,

For all the sickness and pain I had to bear.

I was never alone; you were always there.

I want to thank you for my healing today.

I waited so long with no words left to pray,

But you heard my spirit cry, continued to bless

With your precious love and holy tenderness.

You'll be my master; I will follow your ways,
Lift you up before men, and give you all my praise.
I will heed your command and listen to my call
To spread your gospel truth to one and to all.
I will share your love, what you've done for me,
How you've saved my soul, and set me free.
You've prepared me to be your hands and your feet;
Extend your grace and mercy to all that I meet
When you died for me,
You gave all that you could give.
I will serve you with my life as long as I shall live.

I want to praise you, My Savior,
Give you glory all the time.
I want to thank you, my Redeemer,
Tell the world that you are mine.
I want to give all my worship
To the one who died for me.
I will humble my heart; I will lift up my voice
All the days of my life, I will serve Thee.

Chapter 30

Refined by Fire

"In all this you greatly rejoice, though now for a little while you may have had to suffer grief in all kinds of trials. These have come so that the proven genuineness of your faith---of greater worth than gold which perishes even though refined by fire--may result in praise, glory, and honor when Jesus Christ is revealed."
I Peter 1:6, 7 (NIV)

I am thankful that I experienced all the suffering. Otherwise, I wouldn't be who I am today. Sometimes God doesn't change the situation you are in because He is more concerned about changing your heart. I have learned to yield to my Master and trust that He knows just what I need to mold me into a person that He can use for His kingdom. The following story is one of my favorites.

There was a couple who took a trip to England to shop in a beautiful antique store to celebrate their twenty-fifth wedding anniversary. They both liked antiques and pottery, and especially teacups. Spotting an exceptional cup, they asked "May we see that? We've never seen a cup quite so beautiful."

As the lady handed it to them, suddenly the teacup spoke, "You don't understand. I have not always been a teacup. There was a time when I was just a lump of red clay. My master took me and rolled me pounded and patted me over and over and I yelled out,' Don't do that. I don't like it! Let me alone.'" But he only smiled, and gently said; "Not yet!" Then. WHAM! I was placed on a spinning wheel and suddenly I was spun around and around and around. "Stop it! I'm getting so dizzy! I'm going to be sick," I screamed. But the master only nodded and said, quietly;" Not yet."

He spun me and poked and prodded and bent me out of shape to suit himself and then... Then he put me in the oven. I never felt such heat. I yelled and knocked and pounded at the door. "Help! Get me out of here!" I could see him through the opening and I could read his lips as he shook his head from side to side, "Not yet."

When I thought I couldn't bear it another minute, the door opened. He carefully took me out and put me on the shelf, and I began to cool. "Oh, that felt so good! Ah, this is much bet-ter," I thought. But after I cooled, he picked me up and he brushed and painted me all over. The fumes were horrible. I thought I would gag. "Oh, please; Stop it, Stop it!" I cried. He only shook his head and said. "Not yet!"

Then suddenly he put me back in to the oven. Only it was not like the first one. This was twice as hot and I just knew I would suffocate. I begged. I pleaded. I screamed. I cried. I was convinced I would never make it. I was ready to give up. Just then the door opened and he took me out and again placed me on the shelf, where I cooled and waited-and waited, wondering "What's he going to do to me next?" An hour later he handed me a mirror and said "Look at yourself." And I did. I said, "That's not me; that couldn't be me. It's beautiful. I'm beautiful!"

Quietly he spoke: "I want you to remember, then," he said, "I know it hurt to be rolled and pounded and patted, but had I just left you alone, you'd have dried up. I know it made you dizzy to spin around on the wheel, but if I had stopped, you would have crumbled. I know it hurt and it was hot and disagreeable in the oven, when I brushed and painted you all over would not have had any color in your life. If I hadn't put you back in that second oven, you wouldn't have survived for long because the hardness would not have held. Now you are a finished product. Now you are what I had in mind when I first began with you." Author Unknown

God has a plan and purpose for each of us. He is the potter, and we are His clay. He will mold us and make us, and expose us to just enough pressures of just the right kind so that we may be made into a flawless piece of work to fulfill His good, pleasing and perfect will. He is in complete control of the timing and intensity of your trial. When you endure tremendous pressure in this life with unexplainable peace and joy, the Lord will demonstrate his glorious power to the watching world around you.

I know that God has truly changed my heart to be more like His. This is not something that I could have done through my own efforts. I feel a change, a refining that has come from deep in my spirit. God has answered my prayers and made me into a vessel He can use. I'm certain it will be a continual process for we will never be perfected until we see Him face to face. My suffering has produced a change in my character. As I was meditating, God spoke to me. The Lord said,

"Cheryl, many times when you have a heavy heart, you try to hide it, hoping no one will see or notice. There is need everywhere you turn if you will look and see as I do. See people going about their day, taking care of their business, their families, but are filled with pain and they are hiding it just as you tend to do. Look beyond what you see, Cheryl. Look into their eyes. That is where you will see their soul. I will allow you to see what others do not see. Pain of many kinds is deeply hidden. Sorrow is buried. Discouragement and lies are within the cavity of their being. As I show you these conditions, you must be aware of my Holy Spirit and be in tune to my promptings. Your heart cries for the precious children who hunger and thirst, for families who have lost their loved ones, for children and women in abusive situations, for the poor, for the sick, for the lonely and lost, for the hurting. I have given you my heart and mourning for this world comes with my heart. It is okay to cry when your heart hurts because tears are a part of life and tenderness is an attribute of my heart. I have given you a heart to do my will and to accomplish my purposes. My spirit is with you. Do not be afraid, don't hold back. I have given you your emotions. Compassion and empathy go far in reaching one for me. Never hold back your tears, never hold back what you feel to do and say for I am with you and I have created you to be just who you are."

Chapter 31

Jesus Is the Answer

"Life isn't about waiting for the storm to pass; It is about dancing in the rain." Anonymous

I have shared my story, my heart, my testimony of the power of Jesus Christ. I am only a messenger of His truth. Without His anointing on the words He has given me, they would fail to convey His love and forgiveness to you. Souls are not won to Christ and lives are not changed through persuasive words, but only through the demonstration of the Spirit's power.

He is my all. Without Him, I can't even imagine where I would be. He saved my soul and has brought me through every trial I have ever had to face.

I pray that my story has pointed you to Jesus Christ as the one and only answer to anything you may have to face in this life. May this song He gave me touch your heart and remind you to look to Him.

Look to Me

Cheryl Marie

Look to me when your burdens are too heavy to bear;

Look to me when your mind

Is loaded down with care.

I'll give you victory in me-

Just hold on, I'll set you free

And you'll find life's worth living,

For you're living through me.

Look to me when your heart is broken in two;

Look to me when you're so weary

And you don't know what to do.

I'll give you peace in your soul;

Just hold on and don't let go

And you'll find life's worth living;

This I want you to know.

Look to me when you're crying,
My God, where are you?
I hear your every whisper
And when it's time, I'll bring you through.
Your faith must not waver
Though sometimes you question why.
You'll find all the answers;
Just look to me when you cry.

Yes, you're living in a body
That's a prison to your soul.
There are things that must happen
Before you reach your eternal goal.
But you'll find it's all worth it
For through trials I'll help you grow
Ever closer to me and through everything you will see
That you are stronger and more perfect
Than you used to be.

You'll find life's worth living,
You'll grow closer to me,
Through everything you will see,
You'll find all the answers,

Look to me when you cry,

You'll grow stronger and more perfect

Than you used to be.

I grew up in church and I knew about Jesus and how He died on the cross for my sins. I knew who He was, the Son of God, the Savior of the world. I believed in the Bible. I believed that sin entered the world through Adam and Eve in the garden when they disobeyed God. Because of their disobedience, we "all" inherited the consequences of sin which is death, a spiritual separation from God Almighty.

"For all have sinned and fall short of the glory of God." Romans 3:23 (NIV)

"There is no one righteous, not even one." Romans 3:10 (NIV)

"For the wages of sin is death, but the gift of God is eternal life in Christ Jesus our Lord." Romans 6:23 (NIV)

The price for sin had to be paid. God in His mercy sacrificed His only Son so that we could once again have fellowship with the Father. His blood was shed and was full payment for our sin.

"But God demonstrates His own love for us in this: While we were still sinners, Christ died for us." Romans 5:8 (NIV)

Jesus willingly suffered a cruel death so that you and I could receive salvation and have an eternal home in Heaven. The ransom for all the sin of the world was paid through the shedding of the blood of God's only Son. The agony He suffered and the stripes He bore were for all our sickness and pain.

"But he was pierced for our transgressions, he was crushed for our iniquities; the punishment that brought us peace was on him, and by his wounds we are healed." Isaiah 53:5 (NIV)

Jesus now sits at the right hand of the Father, making intercession for His blood-bought children. His Holy Spirit will guide and comfort us in all situations. His sacrifice was His gift of total redemption to us.

When someone gives you a gift, the first thing you have to do is accept that gift and take it as your own. It is of no benefit or enjoyment to you if you don't accept it or just let it sit unopened. You can look at it and know it's there, but you cannot enjoy or use that gift for its purpose. You must accept and open that gift to reap the benefits.

"God so loved the world that He gave His one and only Son that whoever believes in Him shall not perish but have eternal life" John 3:16 (NIV)

God's gift to us is our unmerited salvation and everlast-ing life through the sacrifice of His Son, Jesus. It is not enough to believe in Christ or have knowledge of Christ's suffering. You must accept His sacrificial gift to you as payment for your sin by openly welcoming the presence of Jesus into your heart and life. Then and only then, can you begin to experience the benefits of His gift to you; His righteousness, His promises, His love, His mercy, His grace, His power, His peace, His comfort, His guidance, His healing, His blessings.

"Here I am! I stand at the door and knock. If anyone hears my voice and opens the door, I will come in and eat with that person, and they with me." Revelation 3:20 (NIV)

Jesus is knocking on the door of your heart right now and he desires to forgive you of all your sins and to wipe the slate of your past completely clean. He desires a relationship with you, to call you His child. He wants to take care of you, comfort you, heal you, and fill you with his peace no matter what happens in this life. He wants to bless you. He is just a prayer away.

Dear Jesus,

I acknowledge that I am a sinner and that you suffered and died in my place to pay the price for my sins and for the sins of the whole world. I accept your gift of salvation. Thank you for your grace and mercy and for sacrificing your life. I openly invite you into my heart and I ask you to dwell in me. I ask your Holy Spirit to fill me with your love. I ask that you would give me your peace and that you would help me to overcome all the burdens of this life. As I experience the darkest valleys, I will trust you to bring me through. I pray in the precious name of Jesus, Amen.

Lord, I Am Nothing

Cheryl Marie

Lord, I am nothing, except for what you've given me;
Like a single grain of sand on the ocean shore, I am.
Lord, I am nothing, but for your mercy and love.
It sweeps over my heart like a rushing wind.
I'm amazed.

Lord, I am nothing,
Compared to your vast and mighty power.
Lord, I am nothing,
In this awesome universe that you've created.
But I stand before you now, enthroned in your grace,
Forgiven and empowered,
I can meet you face to face.

You've created me for worship
And to be a witness for Thee.
May I lift you up so others may see Christ in me.

Lord, I am nothing, but you've poured yourself in me
Like a mighty river flowing through my heart.
I am humbled. I am free.

Chapter 32

Letting Go of the Past

I pray, now that you have read my story, you will know that you are not the only one who has failed God. You are not the only one that has suffered through the storms of this life, many caused by your own wrong choices. You are not the only one that has felt overwhelmed and discouraged, without hope.

There are times when I think about my past and how I would have done some things differently, but I realize that the past is gone. I can't dwell on it; I can't change it; I can't live it again. Satan would have me carry guilt, expound on my failures, and live with regrets, but as a child of God, I am forgiven and free from condemnation.

My faith in God does not carry with it a guarantee of a trouble-free existence on this earth. Tragedies are part of life and they affect the believer and the non-believer alike. Pain and sorrow destroy those who are not grounded in their faith. Life tosses them to and fro and they have no solid ground on which to stand. But those of us who are grounded in our faith, adversity causes us to dig our roots deeper and when the storm rages, we stand firm, unwavering, until it passes over us.

God is able to rescue us from our problems or He may choose to allow us to experience suffering for divine purposes that we cannot understand. Whatever His reason may be, we must endure our hardship, trust the Lord, and yield to His will for us.

None of us have any idea what the future holds. Uncer-tainty is part of life, but there is a sure and solid foundation and that is faith in Jesus Christ. Choose to take a righteous stand as a child of God, reach out in faith, believe in the impossible, expect and receive all God has for you. Choose to be confident in the God who loves you and hears your prayers and answers according to His will. You will have a renewed mind, full of hope, anticipating great things.

Please forgive me. Lord, in the past, I was happy when things went my way and complained when they didn't.

Please forgive me. During these times, I took my eyes off you as my Lord, my Savior, my Protector, my Redeemer, my Healer, my Father, my Hope.

Please forgive me. I doubted instead of trusting you.

Please forgive me. I didn't take note in my heart that you are always in control of all that happens.

Please forgive me. I dwelled on my problems and circumstances instead of keeping my eyes on you.

Please forgive me. I worried more than I prayed.

Please forgive me. I sought an escape in TV and other means of this world instead of reading your promises in your Word.

Please forgive me. I questioned your love, mercy, and grace.

Please forgive me. I allowed Satan to fill my heart with depression and hopelessness.

"I pray, Lord, that you will renew my mind, place a steadfast spirit within me, and fill me with your love and hope. I will stand firm and wait for you to answer my prayers, fulfill my needs, and restore me to the joy of my salvation. I receive all that you have for me. I pray in the precious name of Jesus. Amen"

My heart's desire is to take the lessons I've learned, the strength I've gained, and the testimony I have and impart hope to many people.

Chapter 33

The Sun Will Shine Again

The miseries of my past have become the ministries of my present. God has called me to share my story, to encourage those who are hurting, and to be an example of His miraculous power to heal. The Lord spoke this to me:

"My anointing is upon you to preach, to heal, to disciple, to sing. I will use you mightily. Go and tell of my love, forgiveness, and healing. I will go before you and as you open your mouth to speak, I will give you my words. Do not be afraid to speak. The world may not understand, but those who know me will be blessed. I will equip you to pray and minister salvation and healing to them. Don't be afraid to speak with boldness for the Holy Spirit within you will send forth words from your mouth. Speak those words with confidence for they are my words, not yours. I have called you, Cheryl, to do more than you have dreamed. It is time; step out in faith. I will bless and keep you. Do what I have put in your heart to do. Write your

book, for I am guiding and directing every word. Sing your songs, for the Holy Spirit has given them to you. All the suffering in your life has been for a purpose. Because of your testimony, my kingdom will grow and the lost will be found, the sick will be healed. Share in humbleness and the glory of God will fall upon you. My anointing will flow and miracles will take place."

Healing comes as we turn our lives completely over to the Lord. We must know that He forgives us for the mistakes we have made, therefore, we can forgive ourselves. We also must forgive others who have caused us pain.

The dark clouds that had hovered over me for so many years began to dissipate. The sun's bright rays began to peek through. Slowly the clouds were completely gone and the sky was filled with the brightness of the full sun. Because of God's Son, I once again could experience the brilliance of a life filled with His love and grace and the joy of a life renewed by His Spirit. My dignity and self-worth were restored through the value that God placed on my life. I was free, the heavy weight of all the burdens was lifted from me. God healed me of inflictions of the past, of the torn muscle in my right leg, the oppression, the severe clinical depression, and most recently, the damaged nerves in my right leg.

I heard the voice of Jesus speaking to me as I was meditating on His mercy. The Lord said,

"It is wonderful to stand on this mountaintop with you, Cheryl. It is I who have brought you to this place. Give me all the

glory for it, for it is I who have brought you from the deep and dark places to this bright and beautiful and serene place of peace. You have learned your lessons well. You have praised me and I have heard and set your feet on solid ground. You stood on my Word and the promise that I would never leave you. It hurt me so to watch you suffer for so long, but look at you now! The joy that fills your heart will overflow, the peace and contentment will be seen by those who need it. The enthusiasm to share what I have done for you will be contagious!"

"For his anger lasts only a moment, but his favor lasts a lifetime; Weeping may stay for the night, but rejoicing comes in the morning." Psalm 30:5 (NIV)

The Sun Will Shine Again

Cheryl Marie

The clouds are gathered overhead;

They've been there all too long.

Darkness penetrates the air and gloom is all around.

The thunder sounds, the lightning flashes;

Deep are the floods of pain.

Within my heart, in faith I trust,

The sun will shine again.

And when the sun begins to shine

The Sun Will Shine Again

Don't forget about the night
When Jesus stayed close to your side;
You could feel His presence there.
He held your hand; He wiped your tears;
His strength you had to gain.
With love and trust you knew inside
That the sun would shine again.

Soon and very soon, the sun will shine again.
The storms of life will pass away
And the sun will shine again.
Each passing day the clouds will fade
And the sky will be turning blue.
Keep looking up, He cares for you;
The sun will shine again.

Oh, here it comes; it's breaking through.
Oh, here it comes; He won't fail you!
He won't fail you!

Each passing day the clouds will fade
And the sky will be turning blue.
Keep looking up, He cares for you;

The sun will shine again.

Keep looking up, He cares for you;

The sun will shine again...shine again!

I know in my heart that my victorious recoveries will be an inspiration to you to believe God for anything you need in your life. I would choose to do it all over again just to be able to convince one person that God is able to do the same for them as He did for me. He is no respecter of persons. He loves you and He cares about the trials you are facing. He is a wonderful, loving, and just God who is waiting and longing for fellowship with you, His child.

Through the Holy Spirit, God has given you and me the power to help change someone's world, to tell of the mercies of the Lord, to encourage, to give hope of a brighter day. Smile, be kind, and use the gift of God's victory and wisdom in your life to guide another in the same situation that He has guided you through. We have been lonely, disappointed, sad, discouraged, and hopeless, but because of the love and grace of God, victory is ours! May I encourage you to be a great witness of the love, grace, and power of God.

All thanks and honor and glory goes to none other but the Lord, Jesus Christ. It is to Him I give all my praise for bringing me from the pit of darkness to His wonderful light, from excruciating pain to healing, from utter despair to peace. No words can express my gratitude for His mercy and grace He has extended to me.

"I do not define myself by how many roadblocks have appeared in my path. I define myself by the courage I've found to forge new roads.

I do not define myself by how many disappointments I have faced. I define myself by the forgiveness and the faith I have found to begin again.

I do not define myself by how long a relationship lasted. I define myself by how much I have loved and been willing to love again.

I do not define myself by how many times I have been knocked down. I define myself by how many times I have struggled to my feet.

I am not my pain. I am not my past. I am that which has emerged from the fire." Unknown

All that I was, He brought me from; All that I am today, I owe to Him; All I will ever be is in His hands.

My God is an awesome God, ever faithful, true to His wonderful Word. I will forever give Him all honor, glory, and praise.

"Praise the LORD, O my soul, and forget not all his benefits--who forgives all your sins and heals all your diseases,

who redeems your life from the pit and crowns you with love and compassion." Psalm 103: 2-4 (NIV)

"I will praise you, Lord, among the nations; I will sing of you among the peoples. For great is your love, reaching to the heavens; your faithfulness reaches to the skies." Psalm 57:9,10 (NIV)

As I patiently waited for God to speak to me as to when it was time to release this book, the years brought a lot of changes in my life.

The most significant was the loss, two years ago, of Bill, the love of my life. I took care of him for two and one-half years and watched as cancer devoured his organs and bones. His suffering was horrendous, but he never complained. Hundreds of days were spent in the hospital; continuous chemotherapy, radiation, operations, procedures, ambulance rides, deadly blood infections, hemorrhages, ventilators, pain pumps, and ICU psychosis, but his spirit rallied in victorious peace. I was blessed beyond measure to be his wife and privileged to be his caretaker. Without thought, I did all that was needed to care for and make Bill comfortable. He could do nothing on his own. After he passed, the trauma of watching the man I loved suffer and die affected me greatly. I secluded myself for months and withdrew from family and friends. I was in shock, even though I knew that death was imminent.

One day, Bill asked me to check his shirt because it felt wet. I took him into our bathroom and brought in my piano bench. He was too weak to stand. As I pulled his gray sweat-shirt over his head, I saw his white T-shirt drenched with blood. The day before, the local emergency room had applied a pressure bandage over an incision where a chest tube had been inserted. It had been bleeding, but the doctor assured me that the bandage would stop it. As I removed his bloody T-shirt, the large, saturated pressure bandage fell to the bathroom floor and splattered blood on the white birch cabinets. Blood was gushing from the incision and I couldn't stop it. I had my phone in my pocket and I called Jillian to get help. She came within a few minutes and Shana just happened to stop by as this was all happening. Jillian and I were frantic. Bill was just as calm as ever. Shana applied clean thick pads to the incision and calmly wrapped him tightly with plastic wrap and we were able to get him to the hospital for treatment. After Bill passed, it was difficult to go into that bathroom. For many months, each time I entered, I saw all the blood splashed everywhere and I felt the fear and anxiety of that horrible day. Sadness and grief would overwhelm me.

I couldn't enter the living room of my home without flashbacks of his suffering. This was the room where the hospital bed was, where the morphine pump and the oxygen were used, where I slept on the couch each night with the alarm set every two hours to give medication, where I spent sleepless nights listening for his shallow breaths, where I heard moans and groans of horrific pain, where the nurses examined and cared for him, where friends came to say their last good-byes. This room contained so much pain. I suffered post-traumatic stress symptoms if I even glanced into that room.

I found an amazing Christian therapist who was understanding and specialized in grief counseling. I began to look at my living room differently. This was the room where Bill gave me his last kiss. This was where he whispered "I love you so much and I don't want to leave you." On his last evening on this earth, Jillian, Sheila, and Kay, and I were gathered around his hospital bed. Shana was on her way home from vacation. Bill wanted everyone to leave him and I alone. He looked deep into my eyes and with great effort he whispered, "Where is Shana?" "She will be here soon, Bill," I said. "What is going on?" he questioned. "What do you mean? Because we all are here? We've been here for almost a week, Bill. Everyone's been here, Sweetie," I answered. Bill gazed past me and his large brown eyes circled the perimeter of the ceiling for a few minutes. As the presence of the Lord filled the atmosphere, in awe he whispered, "Not like this." He hesitated for a moment and repeated, "No, not like this." Shivers went down my spine. I didn't see what he saw, but I could feel what he saw and it was glorious. Bill was in heaven by daybreak.

Heaven's Joyful Song

Cheryl Marie

Last night I had a dream that I cannot forget today.

The angels came into my room and carried me away.

I found myself in Heaven

And the light was warm and bright;

I've never seen, nor will ever see

Such a glorious sight!

I stood watching all before me
And I couldn't help but hear
The thunderous sounds of worship
That traveled through the air.
Chills ran up and down my spine
As I watched the heavenly throngs;
Never in my life have heard so beautiful a song.

Praise to Jesus, the Lamb that was slain;
Worthy is our Lord, forever to reign!
Hallelujah to our Master, our everlasting King
Throughout all the ages, your praises we will sing!

I awoke with tears upon my face
His presence I could feel;
I realized it was just a dream,
But it had felt so real!
I'll forever keep the image
Of the place where I had been.
When in doubt or I'm afraid, I'll always think of Him!

He promises He's with me always;
I am not alone.

The one who takes good care of me
Is sitting on the throne.
When in my heart, there is no joy
And things have gone all wrong,
I'll close my eyes and hear again
Heaven's joyful song!

This room is where my wonderful husband was escorted into the arms of Jesus, never to suffer again. Feelings of panic and anxiety when I entered the living room were replaced with a divine peace and reverence. It became "holy ground" to me. I miss Bill more than words can say, but I know he is safe in the arms of Jesus.

Bill had always sat in the chair at the one end of the dining room table. It was just an understood fact that this particular chair at the head of the table was his. No one ever sat in that chair.

When Bill passed, Jillian made a video for the viewing. Marsha, Rose, and Rose's husband beautifully sang the old song, "*Sweet Buelah Land*" as Jillian filmed. At the end of the video, she focused on Bill's empty chair and then a gorgeous blue sky. This impacted me so profoundly that I couldn't look at that chair for months. When our family started to have meals together again, everyone would still leave the chair vacant. I asked that someone please sit in that chair and never leave it empty because it still affects me greatly to this day. Grief never leaves, but I have a Savior who gives me comfort and peace.

Instead of questioning why I only had nine years with this wonderful, kind, caring and precious man of God, my heart was filled with thankfulness and gratitude for the years I shared my life with him. When I married Bill, he taught me how to love and be loved, to trust again, and to be secure and happy in spite of my past. When I cared for him during his sickness, he taught me about faith and steadfastness, about peace and courage, and about complete trust and assurance in knowing our future is with Christ. Yes, Bill taught me how to really live this life. Most importantly, he showed me and those he loved how to die victoriously.

Mom continued to live alone in the house we bought at my graduation. She lived a simple life as she always had. It was apparent that Mom never recovered from the abuse she suffered as a child and with my father. She always had a negative attitude and suffered depression. It frustrated my sisters and I that she wouldn't go to counseling and she did nothing to help herself feel better. We did all we could to make her life happy. She attended church regularly with my sisters, gave her life to Jesus, and was baptized. I was so thankful. We hoped she would find complete peace. She loved spending time with Bill and I. We took her on a few trips with us and we brought her into our home for little vacations as much as she was willing to come. As dementia invaded her brain, she refused to leave her home. We drove the one hundred miles to see her and took her out for dinner as often as we could, but when Bill became ill, our visits decreased. Marsha, Dee, and Rose did a wonderful job caring for Mom when I couldn't. After Bill's death, Mom quickly declined and we all took our turn caring for her. In the final days, it was extremely difficult for me to sleep on the couch in her living room next to her hospital bed, to listen to her breathing, and to give her medication. It brought back so many horrible memories that I had already worked through. I prayed for Jesus to give me the strength to be able to tolerate my days with Mom. Her condition continued to deteriorate and fulltime nurses were assigned. Marsha, Dee, and I no longer carried full responsibility for Mom's care, even though we still had to be present. I could move into the bedroom at night to avoid the circumstances that triggered the post-traumatic stress. As I lay there in her bed, I thought about how thankful I was that Jesus had healed our rocky relationship. I would have no regrets or guilt to carry when Mom was gone. One year after Bill's death, Mom passed peacefully while my sisters and I sang her into heaven. What a beautiful presence we felt even in our grief. God is good!

A Peek at Heaven

Cheryl Marie

Come carry me away up to Heaven's door,
Where I'll live eternally;
And have peace forevermore.

Jesus will be there with his arms held open wide;
He'll say, "Well done, my precious child,
Won't you come inside."

Music fills the air of the heavenly angel band-
Singing like I've never heard
While praising Christ the Lamb.

I see faces everywhere that I can recognize;

My loved ones all surround me
Who knew Jesus when they died.

Emotion overcomes me; joy, it fills my heart
That forever throughout eternity,
I never have to part.

I feel such gratitude; I fall down on my face
Before the feet of Jesus,
I thank Him for His grace.

I'll live forevermore; I understand all things.
His love is overwhelming;
Oh death, where is thy sting?

Marsha, Dee, and Rose also bear the scars of our childhood. Each has had their own struggle to heal their wounded hearts. Their lives today are a testimony of Jesus Christ's love and forgiveness. They have gone on to lead happy and successful lives. We share a beautiful bond, one that no one else can understand, because of what we have endured together. I still feel like a mother to Rose and I love each of them more than they will ever know.

I had no relationship with Scott for fourteen years. After my clinical breakdown, I had to learn to lay him at the feet of Jesus and let go. I thought I had done that, but I continued to cry and beg God to do something. I was not trusting as I should. I took every opportunity to send cards and stay in touch, but was heartbroken when he didn't respond. Finally, I had to release him. God loved him even more than I did. It was one of the hardest and most painful lessons I ever had to learn. Scott's wife became critically ill four years ago. My heart was hurting for him so badly. I prayed and decided to contact him through text and tell him I loved him, I hated that he was hurting so terribly, and I was here for anything he needed. Bill and I contributed a moderate sum of money to help with medical expenses. Scott texted, "Thank you." Those two words were the breakthrough. I attended his wife's memorial, but did not try to approach him. It was difficult not to run to him and console him. It tore me apart to watch him in such pain. A while later, Scott texted me a short note thanking me for the support. That Christmas, he stopped by for gifts from us for his son and we chatted a few minutes and he told me he loved me as he hugged me and left. God was working! Scott came to Bill's funeral and hugged me tight as we cried together. He often sent me encouraging messages as I was struggling with my grief. Because he has been there, he knew just how I was feeling and what I needed to hear. He attended Mom's funeral also and reconnected with the extended family. God is continuing to heal our relationship.

I lost my relationship with Brock about the same time as Scott. My heart was broken for him and how Dan had treated him. *Could he possibly believe that I had told Dan to go to his room and beat him?* I know I had hurt him every time I told him Dan and I were done and shortly after Dan moved back in. *How could a young boy understand the complications of domestic violence when I didn't comprehend them myself?* So many issues in his own life that Brock hadn't worked through had caused additional anger and confusion. Just a few months before the release of this book, my relationship with Brock was restored. My prayers were answered. God is so faithful!

Three months after Bill passed, I was still in shock and withdrawn from everyone. Jillian had asked me to accompany her on a business trip. It was her way of trying to get me out of the house and to help me deal with all the trauma I had experienced caring for my husband. We spent an afternoon enjoying a butterfly atrium and a beautiful flower garden. I commented a few times that I felt unstable and Jillian held onto my arm as we walked through the acres of beautiful flowers. At the end of the walkway approaching the parking area, Jillian instructed me to stand there and wait while she got the car. As she released her grip on my arm and turned to walk away, I hit the ground, smashing my glasses, damaging my teeth, and scraping the side of my face and cheek. In the next three weeks, I fell five more times. After extensive testing, I was diagnosed with Multiple Sclerosis. It has been almost two years since my diagnosis and I have not experienced any additional symptoms. I am trusting the Lord, my life is in His hands, and I have perfect peace.

Shortly after I lost Bill, I was invited to a "Grief Share" group. At the time, I did not choose to attend. I wasn't ready; I needed time to recover. I just wanted everyone to leave me alone. One of my friends called me one day to check on me and told me that she had another friend who became a widow six months before me. She felt we would be good for each other. It had been months and I had been counseling weekly. I knew I had to start putting forth an effort to live life again. I agreed to have lunch with my friend and this widow. In the meantime, while I was waiting for my counseling appointment one day, a woman approached me and called me by name. I thought she looked familiar, but could not place where I had met her. She proceeded to tell me that she knew me from a church that we attended about thirty-three years ago. She used to sit behind me and would also attend concerts that Jillian and I did. She looked familiar, but I really couldn't say that I remembered her. A few days later, I met with my friend and the widow that she told me about. To my surprise, it was the same woman who introduced herself to me days before. We immediately connected as we shared about the loss of our mates. I was surprised that I felt comfortable and trusted her so quickly. We have shared good times and bad. We have shared laughter and tears. We have spent days hanging out and doing just about anything to make life interesting. We have traveled thousands of miles enjoying our adventures. Inseparable ever since the day we met, God surely brought our paths together, once again, at a time when we both needed a good, empathetic, and faithful friend. How wonderful it is to know that He cares about us so much!

Jillian, Shana, and Sheila have had their share of life's struggles physically, emotionally, and mentally. A mother is always concerned about the well-being of her children. No matter what the problem, I have learned to release them to Jesus, who loves them more than I do. I have peace knowing that they are committed Christians, covered in prayer, and nothing can happen to them that God has not allowed.

Marsha, Dee, and I would only see each other on holidays and special occasions for all the years after I moved away. All our visits were with our families and centered around Mom. We took turns and contributed to her care while she was sick. We all made the necessary decisions together at her death. Since then, my sisters and I have made it a point to get together often and are closer than ever.

Dad hadn't spoken to me for over fourteen years. He had no contact with my children or grandchildren. He didn't even care that he had several great-grandchildren that were born since he put us out of his life. He missed weddings, birthdays, operations, household moves, family celebrations, sicknesses, holidays, and funerals. What could I have done to cause such desertion to so many of my loved ones? I will never know. Recently, one of my dad's brothers passed after a lengthy illness. I was close with this uncle and wanted to attend the viewing. Since Dad hadn't spoken to this brother for almost forty years and was at odds with most of his other siblings, I was sure he would not be present. I wondered if I would be welcomed by all my aunts and uncles because of all the distorted stories my dad had told them. I traveled the one hundred miles to pay respects to my uncle. When I arrived to meet Marsha, Dee, and Rose in the parking lot, they informed me that Dad was inside the funeral home. I contemplated leaving, but my sisters and I decided that we would go inside. We had done nothing wrong. Nervously we entered and saw an elderly man sitting on a sofa on the right side of the room. It had been such a long time; I wasn't sure. *Could that be my father?* I was greeted by one of my cousins who informed me that he was indeed my dad. She encouraged me to go to him and give him a hug. "Do this for you. You need to do this, Cheryl, for you." Fear and apprehension froze me as I shook my head negatively. As I glanced toward Dad, his eyes met mine and before I knew what was happening, I found myself with my arms around his neck saying, "Hi Dad, it is good to see you." "It is good to see you, too, Chick," he replied. That is what he used to call me when things were going well. My head was spinning and for once, I had no words to say. I was rescued by another cousin who was nearby. As I chatted, I glanced and saw my sisters, one by one, speaking with the father who had shunned them as he had me. God was doing a miracle right in front of us and my dad's family. Marsha, Dee, Rose, and I shared pictures of children, grandchildren, and great-grandchildren that Dad had deserted for so many years. We answered his questions about our life and our family's lives. Soon the viewing hours had come to an end and it was time to go. Clearly Dad wanted to continue our conversation, but we said our good-byes and left. I thank God for the opportunity to make amends with the father who had caused so much pain, who had tossed me aside like a piece of trash, who put conditions on his love for me, and who had deserted me most of my life. Dad is ninety-four and soon will pass into eternity. I pray that he will think about all the conversations we have had over the years about accepting Jesus Christ. I have peace, now, knowing there is nothing unforgiven and no hard feelings standing between him and I.

God has truly been with me through every chapter of my life. I know that He will continue to work in a mighty way for me and through me. No one knows what lies ahead, but whatever it is, I am ready. Since God has done so many miracles for me, how could I not trust Him for all my tomorrows? When the storms of life come and are raging, I have no doubt, "the sun will shine again."

About the Author

Since the day I surrendered my life to Jesus forty-eight years ago, my heart's desire was use the talents He gave me to serve Him. I was a children's church director, worship leader in several churches, music director, small group leader, and had ministered in the jails and nursing homes. Most of my years were spent traveling with my family's music ministry.

I am an experienced Christian speaker, sharing in churches, organizations, and women's groups. I especially love speaking about my faith, God's goodness and all the wonderful things He has done for me, and about His peace and joy in my life. My message is one of encouragement. The Lord has used my testimony, through word and song, to touch hearts and change lives. It is nothing in myself! I humbly pray that this book has given you the faith to believe in His miraculous power to revolutionize your life as He has mine!

I would love to come and speak at your church, meeting, retreat, or conference and can be contacted through my website.

www.CherylMarie.net

Made in the USA
Columbia, SC
11 January 2020